STEADFAST

OR

STUCK?

Biblical Insights For Breakthrough Leadership

The Best is yet to come!

Damian Smeragliuolo

Published by:

www.hcpbookpublishing.com

ISBN: 978-1-949343-35-9 (paperback)
ISBN: 978-1-949343-36-6 (ebook)

Unless otherwise indicated, all scripture quotations are taken from the New King James Version®. Copyright © 1982 by Thomas Nelson. Used by permission. All rights reserved.

Table of Contents

Dedication

I would like to dedicate this book to my first pastor, Dr. Benjamin Crandall. From the night I received Christ in Calvary Tabernacle in Brooklyn, New York in 1976, he has been a powerful inspiration in my life. His love for the Lord and His Word; together with his gifted ability to bring out of that Treasure things new and old, have modeled leadership that has shaped me. I was watching and I was never disappointed.

In addition, I dedicate this book to every leader in the body of Christ. Your tireless efforts and personal struggles are not unnoticed by the Lord. Many times, you have continued to serve those who follow you while putting aside your personal issues and challenges. I understand all too well; the pressures of leadership and how leaders struggle in silence, together with their spouses and families, paying the price of ministry and often unacknowledged by those you serve. Know that your labor is not in vain in the Lord. Continue to press on toward the prize of the high calling of Christ for your life.

Eternity's morning will tell the tale of all those you have influenced for the Glory of God and the extension of His

Kingdom, whether directly or indirectly. People are watching you. May they see Christ in you and follow you as you follow Him.

The best is yet to come.

Acknowledgment

I once heard a story about a rancher who, while touring his property, noticed a turtle on a fence post. He immediately understood two things about what he saw. Firstly, he didn't know how the turtle got there. Secondly, he knew the turtle didn't get there by himself.

It is the second point that I want to emphasize regarding this book. I couldn't have completed it without the influence of others who encouraged me on my journey.

I would like to thank my wife, Marian, first and foremost. She has been my best friend and lifelong partner for forty-one years. Her faith in God and her encouragement and unshakable confidence in me has never waned. I could never thank her enough.

I would also like to acknowledge others who have influenced me by their example and encouragement. Rev. Elisa Vazquez, whom I have known for over forty years, has been an exemplary model for me. Having authored a book of her own, her example and mentorship has been inspirational and formative to me.

I would also like to thank dear friends, Marty and Pam Richter, Mary Dunham Faulkner and Darcy Anderson for their review of my manuscript and for their encouragement in challenging me to press forward with the book.

I am grateful to Pastor Nancy Aponte of Lighthouse Tabernacle Church in Staten Island, New York, for her encouragement and review of the manuscript as well.

Finally, I would like to thank my dear friend, Evangelist Joan Pearce. I am grateful to her for introducing me to C. Orville McLeish of HCP Book Publishing. His partnership on this project has made it a very smooth and much easier endeavor than I ever anticipated.

May the Lord bless and encourage each one of you for the blessing you have been to me.

Preface

My Classroom

People are my passion.

In over twenty-five years of pastoral ministry, I have had the privilege of walking alongside people of all ages, professions and personalities. I have no greater pleasure than to see people rise to fulfill their potential; grow and develop as secure, fruitful, God-loving leaders in whatever area of life they find themselves.

My passion for people grew partly out of my own journey from childhood. I was born to a woman in crisis. She was married to my father who was an accountant by trade and a functional alcoholic. When he was sober, he was brilliant. When he was drunk, he was nasty and abusive. The cycle of abuse was a surprise to my mother. The rest of his family was well balanced and what anyone would surely describe as successful. She never anticipated the involuntary roller coaster she was forced to ride repeatedly. Her life was a series of alternating repetitions of abuses and apologies and promises to change - punctuated by the statement, "This time I really mean it."

Second, third and fourth chances and hope for change built up only to be dashed to pieces at each turn in the cycle. Finally, she had had enough. Ready to call it quits and file for divorce, she found that she was pregnant with me (and my identical twin brother). What was the prospect of a single mother with two children in the early fifties? Not very good.

Nevertheless, she divorced him. In the process of going back and forth with him making promises she knew he wouldn't keep, her father (my childhood hero) made my dad a proposition. He asked him, "What would it take to get you out of my daughter's life forever?" His response came fairly quickly.

"Fifty bucks," he said.

That was it. He walked out of our lives that day. Within the next couple of years, Mom worked, and my grandparents provided childcare. It was a struggle and I am forever grateful to my family for shouldering the burden together.

A few years later, she met another man related to a cousin in the family. They fell in love and got married. In a short time, he adopted my brother and me. He was a hard worker and a good provider. He was also a functional alcoholic. He had a high school diploma and worked hard.

However, when he drank, he raged. This cycle became the controlling factor in his life ... and ours.

I grew up in a successful family business, working there since childhood with my brother. I learned to work hard. Dad grew up in a tough family and was never nurtured or built up to develop a healthy sense of self-esteem. He developed the business to be a successful and prominent one in our community. His anger, control, strict and demanding ways had a powerful influence on me. I learned to develop a work ethic that has been an invaluable asset to me throughout my life. I also learned to become a perfectionistic workaholic. While I was growing up, the prevailing expression in my family was, "Do the right thing, and you will reap the rewards." I worked hard at that, but the rewards were not always readily forthcoming. So, I learned to work harder and harder; telling myself, "My day will come." But it rarely did.

I didn't discover that I was adopted until I was about thirteen years old. No one in the family ever talked about it up until that time. When I found out, a feeling of satisfaction came over me. I finally understood why I didn't share many things in common with the kind of person my stepfather was. He was the only dad I knew, and I was determined to treat him that way, and with respect. After all, isn't that what all good sons do? I worked hard to make him proud of me, perhaps to repay him for adopting me. I always thought my performance would generate an, "I love you," or "I'm proud of you." They rarely came. Whenever any recognition came, it was second-hand through my mother. She would say, "Your father said you did a great job yesterday." I never heard it from his lips. For some reason, in his mind, he thought that would be a sign of weakness to show emotion or compassion like that. I will always remember the stark contrast between my experience and what I saw on television. On shows like, "Father Knows Best" or "My Three Sons," the father always encouraged their sons and expressed affection toward them, even when they weren't perfect. So, I concluded, there must be something about me that must change. I worked harder.

I was an excellent student throughout my school years: honor rolls, "A" averages and learning how to be a good student while working in the business each day after school and on weekends. We had a good life, but the good days were overshadowed by all the work it took to get to them. I began wondering if it was all worth it. During my years in high school, my dad promised that he would send me to any college I chose. After graduation, I was accepted into a great school in Brooklyn, New York, where (I was told) one in every eleven applicants was accepted. I majored in accounting to benefit the business and please my dad. But after attending for almost a year, he reneged on his promise and told me he wasn't paying my tuition anymore and if I wanted to continue to attend college, I had to go on my own. When I tried to reason with him, reminding him of his promise and my consistent performance, he held his ground. In fact, he fired me and told me to get out of his house, if I persisted in attending college. I left and lived with my maternal grandmother throughout most of my college days.

At the close of my junior year, I had a decision to make. I changed my major to Psychology in my sophomore year and did very well. I was on the Dean's List every semester since that year. Hearing that Psychology majors were driving taxicabs because there was no job market for them, I decided to consider going to medical school. I thought that I would become a Psychiatrist and needed a medical degree to do so. After consulting with the Chairman of the Psychology Department and the head of the Medical School in my college, I planned to move forward. It was in the process of making this decision that my Mom and Dad contacted me to discuss something they had in mind. My dad spoke to me about taking over the business. "After all," he said, "Who am I doing all this for?" So, before taking a step toward committing to five more years of schooling to pursue a medical degree, I decided to take a leave of absence for one year. I thought I would invest that year in the business and determine if the prospect my dad described would truly pan out. It didn't.

After about six months, I began to have conversations with our accountant about restructuring the business to provide concrete steps to bring me into official partnership in the business. I thought that it was time to move from being an hourly employee, to a salaried partner. The accountant thought my proposal was sound and we decided to discuss it with my father the next month. When we did, despite the accountant's efforts to persuade my dad that this was a sure way to go, my dad "lost it." Once the accountant left, he gave me an ultimatum, "If you think you could do better on your own, then get out and do it," he said. I realized then that I would be stuck there with no plan or prospect, so I left. I worked every job I could find to make money while living with my maternal grandmother again. It was difficult, but at least I was venturing out to carve my own path.

A year later, he asked me to come back, and I did. He made promises of partnership and drafted up the necessary papers. That day never came. After about six months, I was invited to attend a non-denominational church service by a friend. I had always attended church, having grown up as a Roman Catholic. The service I attended was so different. After hearing the young man preaching that evening, I decided to surrender my life to

Jesus Christ and became a born-again Christian. My life was transformed! Even though I couldn't explain it in detail, I knew something had happened.

After six more months of working in the family business, another crisis arose. My parents were not in favor of my newfound faith and thought I was being brainwashed. So, my dad came to me with another ultimatum. He wanted me to quit going to "that church." When I tried to explain what had happened to me, and the joy I found in my experience, he pressed the issue. He said, "You have ten days to quit that church. If you don't, you're fired, and I will need you to get out of the house and give me back the truck I bought you." Ten days came, and I left; heavy hearted, and empty handed.

It has been a challenging road over these last forty or so years. I have learned many things during that time. The good news is that, eventually, my entire family came to Christ and our relationships were reconciled and maintained better than they had been in years. I also had the opportunity to meet my biological father and reconciled. One of the greatest blessings in my life was to connect with his whole side of the family. Over the years, he became involved in the Salvation Army. Both dads are in heaven now, and I am so thankful to the Lord for that assurance. I have grown in my journey in many ways.

Forty-one years ago, I married a wonderful woman, my best friend and the love of my life. We have three adult children and five grandchildren. Eventually, I answered the call to pastoral ministry and function in that role to this day.

Why am I sharing this with you? Simply to say that I know what it's like to be "stuck" in a place that I know I don't belong any longer. I understand the pressures, frustrations, questions, and inner wrestling that occurs for all who find themselves stuck at various times in their lives. I have learned to use my own journey as a classroom for my personal development and growth. I am persuaded that your own journey can be a classroom for you as well.

This book came about from hundreds of hours of pastoral ministry counseling and walking alongside gifted people striving to always do their best to live satisfying lives that make an impact on the lives of others. I believe the Bible is the Word of God and contains all that we need "...for life and godliness" (See 2 Peter 1:3). In this light, I have cited the lives of several people and leaders found in the Bible as models for us of what to embrace, and what to avoid in our journey toward growth and personal development.

It is my hope and prayer that you will find things you may identify with as you discover that our Biblical heroes are just regular people with problems and flaws just like us, and, like us, they were challenged to become all they could be, with God's help. I trust you will find some light in the following pages that will illuminate some of the dark areas in your life that you may not have desired to look into before or did not know how.

I suggest you read each passage of Scripture referenced in each chapter prior to reading the chapter. Ask the Holy Spirit to shed light on any area of your soul where you share what the person in the chapter experienced. I am confident that as you discover and apply the suggested steps outlined, you will come to a place of healing, freedom and restoration that will produce lasting, impactful fruit in your life and those you serve.

The best is yet to come.

INSIGHTFUL PROFILES IN BIBLICAL LEADERSHIP

Profile One: Are You Steadfast Or Stuck?

Overcoming A Victim Mindset And The

Blame Game

Key Scripture: John 5:1-9

Change: no one likes it, but everyone must learn to experience and manage it. Many years ago, in speaking about change, a colleague of mine said, "Constant change is here to stay." I have thought about the wisdom of that statement very often over the years. It prepares us to be ready for change whenever it is needed - and it will be needed. When we respond creatively to change in a timely manner, the results are what we call success. The ability to be adaptable, to anticipate needs and create new solutions in evolving circumstances are core characteristics of influential and effective leaders.

Most leaders make observations within the organizations in which they serve and attempt to discern where change may be needed. We take assessments, create SWOT analyses and change policy and procedure manuals to get things done more effectively and efficiently. This kind of change is what most of us are used to and have the most experience with. It may not be easy, but we seem to be able to shift as needed to reach our goals and make improvements whenever change is needed in the environment around us. However, it is quite another thing to make observations and cite changes that need to be made within us. In fact, many of us never perceive what changes need to be made within us. We often simply lack the objectivity. In addition, we may have fallen into the habit of continuing to do things a certain way. Our training, the examples of those who mentored and taught us and what our peers have modeled for us often keep us from seeing what may be so obvious to others. Namely, we need to change. Failing to realize this need, coupled with our determination to do things the same way we have done them for so long keep us stuck. We may perceive ourselves as being steadfast, dependable, faithful and determined. We continue to press on, doing things in the same ways, expecting results to come with just one more push. "After all," we tell ourselves, "This is how I was trained; this is the right way to do it." In this mindset, when hoped-for results are lacking, we look outward for something (or someone) else to blame.

Our friend in the Key Scripture (John 5:1-9) illustrates a person who had found himself stuck. He was in the right place. He was doing the best he could. He knew what needed to be done to get unstuck. He tried to better his situation, only to fail repeatedly. He knew that change was needed, and he desperately sought it. But when continually disappointed, he looked to his surroundings for reasons (and people) to blame for being stuck. Let us take a look at this man's plight for more insight.

The unnamed man was sick. He had gone to Bethesda because there was an opportunity to get healed of his ailment. It was a place where supernatural healing took place periodically. However, he couldn't meet the conditions for healing. When an angel from the Lord would disturb the waters, the first one into the pool at Bethesda would get healed. He remained there determined to get his opportunity. He was motivated and worked hard to meet the conditions that would bring success. But he could never get into the pool on time. Someone else always got there before him. He missed his chance repeatedly. He was sick for thirty-eight years.

Thirty-eight years is a long time. No doubt it seemed longer than that, especially for the man who occupied a place on a porch at Bethesda. While we don't know how long he was on the porch, we do know that he had been sick for a long time. I suppose after being sick all those years, every failed attempt to get well made it seem longer. It is a long time to struggle to get into position to get well. It is a long time to want something so badly, only to be disappointed repeatedly in your efforts to obtain it. It is a long time to see others get their breakthrough while you still wait to get yours. It is a long time to be --- STUCK!

This nameless man at the pool is identified for us only by the circumstances in which he found himself. He was in a place surrounded by other sick people. He was "hospitalized" when we meet him in Scripture, always trying to reposition himself to get well. In short, he was identified to us by what he lacked. He was identified by his "problem." We don't know who he was. Was he a tax collector, lawyer, doctor, or undertaker? What were his skills, abilities and gifting? Was he a leader?

What Is A Leader?

A leader is a person who is in charge of some organization comprised of others. He or she is responsible to give direction, train, teach, encourage and guide the group toward accomplishing desired outcomes and goals for the organization. The organization in which a leader is involved may be a ministry, corporation, department or even a family. On one hand, a leader may be the person with the title of CEO, President, or Manager formally assigned to lead a group. On the other hand, a person may occupy the position of leader informally. In other words, the person has attained a level of influence over others in directing them towards achieving desired behaviors and accomplishing organizational goals. By the definition used here, almost all of us can qualify as a leader in some capacity. This means that any one of us can find ourselves stuck at some stage of our lives and need to discover how to break free.

The passage is silent on the status of this man. Nevertheless, he shares a condition with many leaders in the church and in the marketplace today. Let me explain.

There are many leaders who are "stuck" on their own porch in their personal "Bethesda." They have had dreams and visions of ministry or their careers and all they planned to accomplish. But all their hard work, best intentions, sacrifices and exercise of their skill sets have not accomplished what they hoped they would. They have tried to get themselves out of their "stuck" condition by repositioning themselves time and time again. They have attended seminars, classes, webinars, retreats and all sorts of promising remedies, only to be repeatedly disappointed.

We always begin our repeated attempts at repositioning ourselves with an expectation that it won't take long, but it often does. This is where the frustration sets in. This is where bitterness can set in. This is where the temptation to quit takes root.

Missing Your Season

Can you imagine the hope that was in this man's heart when he first went to Bethesda? I am sure he planned and envisioned what it would be like when he was the first one into the pool after the angel moved the water. When he missed the first one, he undoubtedly galvanized his resolve and set his goal to not miss the second one. Missing the second one, I am sure he tripled his determination to make it the next time. He may have missed two, but there was no way he would miss a third. I wonder at which point he just decided to give up and stop trying? Thirty-eight years of missing his opportunity, his season, changed something in him. He became cynical. He started to look for others to blame for his circumstances. I am sure he may have thought, "Why do I always miss my opportunity, while others experience theirs?" I suspect he looked around at those who were better positioned than he was. Perhaps he looked with disdain at those closer to the pool than he was. *Was that last person to get into the pool more physically capable than I was? Why them and not me?* I wonder if he began to look at himself when there was no one else left to blame?

When we miss our seasons, we too may struggle with the feeling of frustration for being stuck in a place we really don't want to be. However, circumstances have caused us to be there, and we cannot wait to get out of that place as soon as possible. But when things don't change and persist for a protracted period of time, we can become angry. We can become embittered. We can begin to play the "blame game."

The Victim Mindset

When we have experienced repeated disappointments and our plans have been frustrated again and again, blaming others for our plight, we can fall into the trap of developing a victim mindset. A mindset is a certain perception that we maintain, especially of ourselves. We filter everyone and every circumstance around us through it. Our mindset determines how we either respond or react to things. When we have a victim mindset, we perceive ourselves as always being abused somehow. We see other's around us as the abusers. We react to things and people rather than respond to them. We react destructively out of our hurt, rather than respond constructively from a healthy perspective. The man in our story didn't respond to Jesus; he reacted to Him.

Jesus asked him an all-important question, "Would you be made whole?" The man's reaction was, "I have no one to help me." He further complained that inevitably someone else would get into the pool ahead of him. There is an implication here that he did possess some ability to get to the water, but his focus was on someone else as the reason why he wasn't having success in his efforts to be whole.

There he remained. He was stuck with no one to help. His mindset prevented him from accurately evaluating his situation and discerning a clear path forward.

Many leaders, like this man, find themselves stuck. He was in a repeated process bouncing between hope and disappointment that caused him to lose objectivity and become enslaved in the cycle of being victimized by people and by circumstances. There are leaders today in the church, and in the marketplace, in the same condition as this man. They have tried, time and time again, to reach their goal, only to be repeatedly disappointed. Why? They don't have enough money; they don't have the right staff; they never catch the right breaks; they never make the connections that others seem to come by so easily that will help facilitate their success. All their efforts are never perceived as the problem. It is always someone or something else's fault. In short, "They have no man."

The rut that this victimized man is in is deeper than we may realize at first. Not only is he stuck in his place on the porch, but he is also trapped by the self-deception that he has done all he could to better himself. His condition has not improved, and it seems he is further away from his goal than he ever was. Busy-ness had misled him to think that he was doing something about improving his predicament. He kept trying again and again to get whole but failed every time. His repeated efforts surely made him feel that he was doing all he could. Many leaders make the same mistake. They miss their goals repeatedly and apply more effort and energy the next time around, only to end up in the same place repeatedly. They want change but rely on what they have always done to get it, believing somehow that this time, it will work. They determine to work harder but fail to see their need to work smarter. When external circumstances don't change, despite all our efforts to succeed, it may be that we need to seek change within ourselves.

Would you be made whole?

Jesus' question to this man is a penetrating one. When a person has been stuck in the same situation year after year, he can become so accustomed to it that he learns to live with it. It becomes his new "normal." Plans, efforts, energy, and money spent on getting to our goals keep being expended, but we are no closer than we were before. We are caught in a vicious cycle.

Jesus didn't ask the man if he thought he COULD be made whole. He asked if he WOULD be made whole. There is a difference. Jesus wasn't asking about his capacity to be whole; He was challenging his desire to be whole. He was asking if he had had enough! While we may think that the answer to the question is a no brainer, it apparently wasn't for him. It may not be for us. Why? I suggest two reasons for why this is a challenge for many. Firstly, we must admit and acknowledge that we need to change. Secondly, we must take responsibility in taking the necessary steps to begin the process for change. Jesus was challenging this man. He wanted to know if he was ready to accept the responsibility and take the action necessary to be made whole, rather than stay where he was.

The Responsibility Of Being Whole

What we find so troubling about change has to do with our expectations. It is easy to expect change from others. We can cite specific areas that need to change. We can help map out steps to follow that will aid in the process. We can encourage, admonish, exhort and even correct someone else in his or her journey toward change. But when it comes to change in us, we hit a wall. It is painful when this happens. This is especially true for someone who has struggled with a victim mindset. Why? Because we think we are being forced to admit that there is something wrong with us. We shrink back from the thought that "I" may be the problem. This is nothing more than the flip-side of a victim mindset. A victim has pointed the finger towards others as the reason for their struggle; blaming, accusing and labeling them (if only in their minds) as bad people for so long. The thought of pointing a finger toward myself must mean that I too am a bad person. NOT TRUE!

Emotionally healthy leaders don't have a problem looking within to make assessments for where change is needed. They aren't afraid of other people's opinions of them. They don't have unrealistic expectations of themselves or others. They realize that people aren't perfect and that includes them. They have the ability to let themselves off the hook and realize that everyone needs to change from time to time. This enables them to confront areas needing change and to embrace the process necessary to accomplish it. This is a normal, healthy process of thinking that may be challenging for someone who has struggled with a victim mindset.

There will be expectations of him that no one had while he was stuck on the porch. There will be no one else to blame for staying stuck. An emotionally healthy leader will need to plan, think, and evaluate new ideas and methodologies that he never had to think about when he was stuck on the porch. An emotionally healthy leader may need to work with a team of others in order to achieve his goals toward change. This means that others would see his strengths, and his weaknesses. An emotionally healthy leader allows him or her to become vulnerable.

Vulnerability will enable him or her to be open to correction, criticism, healthy conflict, negotiating, and sharing authority with others. An emotionally healthy person becomes willing to share his success with others. In short, to be an emotionally healthy person requires taking risks he or she never had to take before.

I suspect that all these thoughts flashed through the mind of this man when Jesus asked the question. The Scripture doesn't record an answer. What would your answer be? Are you stuck on a porch in your life? Are you expending hours of time, energy, strength and other resources to achieve your goals, only to not reach them again and again? Are you tired of the frustration and disappointment of spending financial, physical and emotional capital while staying stuck in the same place year-in and year-out?

Take The Control Back From Your Mat

Let us consider the man's mat for a moment. It was what he laid on every day, all day. It was the place he went back to time and time again after each failure to getting unstuck. It identified where he was. This was his spot. It also identified who he was. It became an inseparable part of his life. His mat was the controlling factor in his life. How did it get control? No doubt it happened the moment the man accepted the conclusion that this was the way his entire life would be. From that point on, he resigned himself to living with it indefinitely. He could never imagine a life without that mat. He derived a certain sense of security living on that mat, even in negative circumstances.

Do you have a "mat" in your life? Is there a condition or circumstance that you have resigned yourself to live with forever? Is it a job, a title, someone else's expectations of you? Are you stuck somewhere, accepting your place on the porch, while something inside you cries out for more? Have you given up on your dreams for the future and your passion to accomplish something significant because the mat has all the control in your life?

Repeated failure and years of deferred hope can have that effect on leaders. We become so accustomed to telling our story from the viewpoint of what we don't have; what we are missing; our problem, that we surrender all control to that condition. Now, that condition rules. It determines our current state and, more destructively, our perception of our future as well. Yes, the mat was the problem. It represented the embodiment of his situation, and he desperately wanted to be rid of it forever! But remember, he had no man to help him.

When a leader, or anyone, has been stuck in the same fruitless, crippling situation year after year, we become "comfortable" with it. Being stuck in the same place of stagnation (personally and occupationally) can cause us to surrender control to the problem. It becomes the embodiment of our entire lives. We become the victim. The job is the problem; the pastorate is the problem; the people are the problem. It is because of them that I am stuck. If only I can get rid of this "mat," my troubles would be over. If only I can change location. If only I can get out of pastoring. If only I could get rid of this mat. Jesus was challenging the man to roll up his mat: to regain control for change in his life. We must not let the "mats" in our lives wield control over us.

Jesus challenged him to do something he probably would never have done. Jesus didn't heal the man and afterwards tell him to pick up his mat. He commanded him to "stand up, pick up your mat and walk." This challenged the man's thinking. After all, Jesus wouldn't ask him to do something he was incapable of doing, would He? That is the point. He was capable and he did it!

We often look to others to be the catalyst for change in our lives and circumstances. Like this man stuck on the porch, we are constantly looking around in the hope of spotting someone who can help. What I believe Jesus did in this man's life was to challenge him to believe that the catalyst for change was him. He came to the place where he realized that he had to initiate the first step toward change. When he did, he discovered that he was healed! Once we take the first step, all the other parts in the process of change take place.

Where are you in this story? What is keeping you stuck in a fruitless cycle of repeated failed efforts? Are you suffering from a physically crippling disease or an equally crippling unseen condition of a victim mindset? Either one can keep you stuck for years.

There are three steps in Jesus' command to this man. He told him to, "stand up, pick up your mat, and you will walk." Let us examine this prescription for the man's breakthrough.

Stand Up

The first thing we need to understand about this command is that Jesus would not have asked him to do something he was incapable of doing. The challenge for the man was "rolled up" in what he thought he was capable of doing! Somehow, a "switch" was thrown inside the mind and heart of this man when he heard Jesus' words. He believed. This faith enabled him to stand up.

Standing up requires that we think of ourselves differently than we have before. Instead of thinking of ourselves based on our inability, we must be challenged to think about ourselves based on our capability. Instead of drawing conclusions about ourselves (and our situation) based on our past failed efforts, we need to think about ourselves based on our future potential. A "switch" needs to be thrown inside of us where we become determined to take action. Let us think for a moment about when we started out in leadership. I am certain that our actions were based on a promise that may have inspired us. We had a dream, a vision, a hope. We launched out, we ventured, we tried. That spark is still resident within our hearts right now! Being stuck for so long may have veiled that spark, but it has not extinguished it. It wasn't extinguished in this man either. This spark was all Jesus needed to re-ignite hope for change in this man's heart. It was all Jesus needed to re-connect this man with his original dream and vision. It was all this man needed to begin the process of restoration.

What about you? Take a few moments to think back on your own journey. Imagine the potential, the vision, the hope you had which seemed to be enough for you to launch out. I am convinced that you will find that it is all you need now to re-launch! Furthermore, consider this: Jesus knew the day He called you that the days of being stuck would come. Your present situation doesn't negate His original calling and commission. So, stand up!

Pick Up Your Mat

Once we have stood up, we need to be determined to take back control and take action. Register for that new course. Finish your degree. Start researching what you need to do to accomplish your dream. Reach out to people who are doing what you really want to do with your life. Determine that you will help someone else achieve his or her dream and you will achieve yours. Re-ignite your passion for what makes you excited to get up each morning.

Here is something every leader must realize if he would become whole. The thing that hurt (crippled) you will be the thing God uses to heal you. What do I mean by this? Well, you were given certain gifts, abilities and capacities by God to fulfill your destiny. When Jesus asked the man to pick up his mat, he was directing him to regain control over the mat, rather than having the mat control him any longer. He didn't tell him to throw the mat away. He directed him to get a hold of it. He empowered him to have authority over his situation, not allowing his situation to have authority over him any longer. Just as the mat really wasn't the problem, neither is the job, the pastorate, the people, the church or any other "mat" regardless of what form it is represented in your life. This is a crucial revelation for all leaders stuck on a porch. Without such a revelation, leaders will tend to run away from the very thing they were gifted and called to do.

If a church hurt you, God will use a church to heal you. If a pastor hurt you, God will use a pastor to heal you. If a bishop hurt you, God will use a bishop to heal you. If a leadership network hurt you, God will use a leadership network to heal you. If your position of leadership hurt you, God will use your position of leadership to heal you. It is time to regain a right perspective on your "mat." It is time to regain control and maintain a healthy mindset toward your gifting, calling, and capacity and fulfill your God-given potential to finish the race you began, even if it was thirty-eight years ago. That leaves only one thing left to do ---

Walk

It is time to do a 360!

The word interpreted "walk" carries the connotation of "going full circle." Not only did this man need to move from where he was to where he was going, but I believe the connotation of going "full circle" has a particular

42

significance here. I believe it implies that he was to get back to a new beginning; to where he was when he started. Think about it. If he were only to do a 180, he would change his direction, but only from his present state and toward an opposite one. A 360 would bring him back to the beginning, when he had something that he did not possess in his present condition. When he began, he didn't have an illness, he didn't have shame, he didn't blame, he wasn't a victim. I believe he needed to recapture his original dreams for his life. He needed to recapture his original hope, zeal, and excitement and yes, his faith that he began his journey with.

What About YOU?

If you are stuck on a porch today, it is time for a new beginning; it is time for a fresh start. Wait on the Lord today, and when you sense His presence, listen for His word of instruction to you. Like this man, you can hear His word despite your present condition! He will speak to you in terms you will understand, are capable of accomplishing and that you will not miss or require special revelation to understand. I am certain that His instruction to you will include some form of, "stand up, pick up your mat and walk!"

You may be thinking, "Well, not everyone on those porches got healed that day." This is the same victimized thinking that will keep you stuck. The KEY in this situation is that regardless of what happened to anyone else who was stuck in Bethesda, the man himself was healed. I am glad that this man is unnamed in the story. I suggest that you place your name in the story. This man wasn't a nobody: he was anybody. What Jesus did for him, He could do for you too.

Each of us, who are stuck, needs to answer the question, "Would you be made whole?" What is YOUR answer?

Hear the Word of the Lord to you:

Stand up: Believe that the sacrifice of Jesus on the cross has given you the opportunity to be healed completely inside and out.

Pick Up Your Mat: Don't let your circumstances have the control any longer. What God says about you determines the outcome of your life, not your circumstances. Understand that God will use what hurt you to heal you.

Walk: Finally, start over and move on to fulfill your destiny and have joy in the journey.

There were two healings this man experienced. One was physical, affecting his body; the other was spiritual, affecting his soul. Both are possible for you today, if you need them.

Profile Two: The Philippian Jailor

How Codependency Ensnares Leaders In Unsuspected Bondage

Key Scripture: Acts 16:16-34

There is a term that has gained a certain level of acceptability and popularity in church culture. It is the term, "wounded healer." While it may be intended to convey the idea that none of us are perfect, or an attempt to identify with those we are trying to lead, let us examine it more closely.

We must ensure that woundedness doesn't become an excuse to justify negative and unacceptable behaviors in leaders at any level. Instead, we must become "healed healers" in the Body of Christ. Let me explain.

No one has to be perfect to lead. No one has to be flawless and constantly victorious in order to feel qualified to lead. In fact, victory over our own struggles with sin and other negative behaviors actually qualify us to serve those going through similar experiences. However, we must be sure that the wounds we experienced in the past have now become scars. A scar is a healed wound. It is no longer bleeding, but restored to original condition prior to when the wound was experienced. Therefore, the most equipped (and equipping) leader is one who bears the scars of experiences he have worked through but is no longer hurting in those areas. Hurt people hurt people. Healed people heal people.

Codependency

Many leaders have survived living in families where there has been someone struggling with an addictive behavior. Those ministering to families who have been damaged or destroyed through drug or alcohol abuse know fully well the toll it can take on the rest of the family. In fact, many leaders in the body of Christ today can look back and recall the day they vowed, *"I will NEVER drink alcohol or take drugs,"* etc. They will never abuse their spouses, children or themselves in ways they experienced in childhood. They will never be "that person."

However, growing up in a family like this often has an impact that is not readily discernable. The condition is called "codependency." The definition of codependency is: *"A psychological condition or a relationship in which a person is controlled or manipulated by another who is affected with a pathological condition (such as addiction to drugs or alcohol); broadly speaking, it is dependence on the needs of, or control of another."*

The codependent person growing up under the influence of this "cycle of addiction" has become accustomed to living out this cycle, by default, with the addicted person. The cycle of addiction moves from pain to anesthetic; from anesthetic to pain; and from pain to anesthetic. This occurs repeatedly, in a downward, spiraling cycle. It takes more "anesthetic" to deaden more "pain" at each turn in the cycle. The codependent person, while never becoming addicted to the "anesthetic" of drugs or alcohol, ends up adopting the same cycle of addiction. The only difference is, they have opted for a more acceptable form of anesthetic.

For example, the child of an alcoholic or drug addict may grow up becoming a workaholic; a spend-aholic; a rage-aholic; a sex-aholic and even a church-aholic. While keeping their vow never to repeat a behavior they grew up with, they fall into the same cycle of addiction, only with a more acceptable form of "drug." They simply continue the addiction, only replaced with another behavior. You see, workaholics usually get the promotions. However, their marriages often fail, and their families become destroyed in the process. When feeling the same basic "pain" of low esteem, feelings of inadequacy or inferiority, the codependent turns to his "drug of choice." The "drug" becomes any other behavior that is intended to deaden the pain they are feeling. Here is the key fact about any addiction; the element of addiction is not the behavior itself, but the control that is at the core of the behavior and the reason for its continuance. The codependent doesn't have a need for drugs or alcohol but does have a need for control. This is what drives their behavior.

Five Signs of Codependency

1. An inability to say, "No."

In any normal personal transaction, we may feel some sense of anxiety when we have to say "No" to someone.

For the codependent, it is almost impossible to do so without creating extreme levels of anxiety at the thought of non-compliance. This person usually takes on too many responsibilities to handle effectively.

2. Prioritizing other people's needs at the expense of your own.

Codependents have a deep desire to help others and a need to feel needed. They typically help too much, certainly more than the person they are trying to help is willing to accomplish. Usually, these people answer questions no one is asking. There is a powerful drive to feel needed, as well as to build an identity based upon the approval of others.

3. Low self-esteem and shame.

They don't think they deserve to have their needs met and usually feel guilt over something they have done or may not have done but feel they should have. Often, they have a sense of shame, which is feeling bad about who they are, rather than feeling guilt over what they have done. As a result, they often suffer through guilt, shame and overwork, thinking that this is somehow being "Christ-like."

4. Issues with control.

This is a central issue for the codependent because it represents power over another party. Addicts often manipulate and control others through physical and emotional abuse. This leaves their victims powerless and helpless, making it easier to control them. Victims of abuse (that is, codependents) also use control in order to manipulate others. Whether it is rank, title or having any level of authority over others, codependents in leadership often manipulate others to satisfy their need for control. By using guilt, shame, and other tactics, they pressure others into compliance with their wishes. They may use the threat of rejection or giving or withholding approval as means of soliciting compliance. This use of manipulation for control is as equally abusive as the addict's abusive use of control. Sadly, this, too often, is allowed to persist because it is not readily recognized as abuse to the average person. Many times, the victim of abuse thus becomes the abuser.

5. Mood disorders.

Codependents shoulder an enormous emotional burden regarding themselves. Anger, fear, anxiety and depression are often the result and become evident in their behavior. People living (or working) with this type of leader now become enmeshed in the same addictive cycle of control. This becomes a threat to the well-being of the team, as well as the organization, and must be identified, confronted and eliminated.

Let's turn to the story of the Philippian Jailer to see how these traits are evident in his life. While we usually concentrate on the experience of Paul and Silas in this passage, we will focus on the jailer for some thought-provoking insights into his behavior. The key element I want to focus on regarding the jailer is *the issue of control.*

Paul and Silas were imprisoned as a result of casting a demon out of a slave girl that earned lots of money for her masters. You could say she was a medium or fortune-teller. Unlike many in this profession, this woman actually knew things, and that element of truth (as part of a larger lie) was what kept people coming to her. They paid for her services and it was the loss of this economic profit to her owners that became a problem.

The Pressures and Urgency of the Moment

In Acts 16:19-21, we see that the owners of the slave girl brought Paul and Silas before the local authorities, accusing them of wrongdoing. They told the authorities that the whole city was in an uproar because of what Paul and Silas had done. Bear in mind, they didn't say the exorcism was wrong. They claimed Paul and Silas were preaching and teaching things that were wrong. In addition, they emphasized that what they had done was "illegal," teaching customs that Romans were forbidden to practice. A mob formed. Paul and Silas were severely beaten and thrown in prison. The jailer was ordered to be sure they didn't escape. So, the jailer put them into the deepest, darkest part of the prison, the inner dungeon.

It is not difficult to imagine the pressure the jailer felt. This was a public issue. It impacted the economy. City officials and prominent, tax-paying businessmen's livelihoods were at stake. The pressure must have been quite intense on this jailer, so he "buried" Paul and Silas deep in the prison. He just couldn't afford to let these two "problems" escape (See Acts 16:24).

Codependent leaders struggle with pressures much like this jailer. Various issues in their lives - some secret sin, some moral failure or fear of failure, some past rejection that they don't want to repeat again – are kept deeply "buried" inside. Not only do they not want to remember them, but they also do not want anyone else to discover them. They are all kept in the deepest, inner "dungeon" of their hearts and souls.

As with the jailor, it is not too difficult to imagine the pressure and anxiety created by the thought of them "getting out": "What if people find out what's really deep inside me," the codependent fears; "I can't look like I have a problem. After all, I am the one charged to prevent and resolve everyone else's problems." How does the codependent leader avoid having his inner fears escape? He uses CONTROL to keep the problems locked up. You see, the warden was as imprisoned as much as those he ruled over. He lived in prison daily. He didn't become imprisoned in the ways the other prisoners were, but he was still imprisoned WITH them. This is classic codependence.

The Codependent's Self-Deception

It is important to realize that this jailer was a leader. He was the warden of the prison. He had serious responsibilities. His actions impacted the welfare of the city and society in which he lived. He had authority, rank and a certain level of respect, at least as much as a warden should expect. He *had the keys in his possession to prove he was in control.* Like many codependents in positions of leadership, he practiced a form of self-deception. His two "problems" were locked up tight. He was in control and the sound of the keys jingling on his hip confirmed his perception every time he heard them. Herein lies the deception; *just because you have the keys, doesn't mean you're okay and not imprisoned.* The issues you have locked deep in some inner dungeon of the soul are not under your control. They are actually controlling you.

I realize this is an extremely sensitive and potentially alarming statement. However, it nevertheless describes many in leadership in churches today. For example, in over twenty-five years of pastoring, I have heard from leaders' wives asking for prayer for their abusive husbands. When I asked if he would be willing to speak to his pastor, the spouse revealed, "Well, that is challenging as he is one of the church's deacons." Emotionally and verbally abused spouses and children of ministers know all too well the pressure of manipulative statements made by their *abusers: "You're the pastor's kids, so you'd better not ever get into trouble"; "You're the preacher's kid and you must set a good example"; "What will people think if my wife doesn't meet the expectations of the deacons? I could lose my job"; "If you really loved the Lord, you would understand the pressure I'm under and help me, no matter what."* I could go on…

All these statements are manipulative, controlling and abusive. Leaders who find themselves making them on a consistent basis need to find help and be set free from their addiction to control. However, control is not always exercised in terms of making statements like those cited above. Often, control is demonstrated more subtly in the form of perfectionism. While we should all strive for excellence in ministry, and do our level best for the Lord and His people, perfectionism is a harsh taskmaster and can drive leaders to become abusive.

Perfectionism is often fueled by the fear of failure, fear of rejection, the need for approval or the need to feel adequate and competent. Leaders who battle codependency often mask their attempts to control by making statements that appear harmless on the surface but are, in fact, manipulative. By doing this, they force those they lead to be *painted into an emotional corner,* so their only way out is by compliance. They use statements like: *"Well, I know we all have family responsibilities, but this is ministry."* Another tactic is to say, *"Well, what would others think if I let you show up when it's convenient?"* Or, *"If this isn't done with excellence, my reputation as a leader will be sullied"* (with the implication that it would be your fault)! Here is a big one: *"After all I've done for you, I ask this one thing and you don't have time for me?"* There are other statements like these that are used. Many leaders struggling with codependency may not even realize they are being so manipulative and abusive.

Sheep need to be led, not driven. Staff members need to be led, not driven. Families need to be led, not driven. Healthy ways of thinking and communicating are what these leaders need to work diligently at accomplishing. This is why the scriptures teach us to "...let our yes be yes, and our no be no..." (See Matthew 5:37).

We must practice saying what we mean and meaning what we say. It may sound too simple, but it is a start. Remember, just because you have the title, the position, the experience, the responsibility, anointing, the KEYS, doesn't mean you are not bound-up somewhere deep inside.

The jailer was in prison every single day of his life. This bondage served to keep the jailer from experiencing something the other prisoners were able to. They heard Paul and Silas singing and worshiping God from the dungeon. Wow, God was actually moving in the prison and it woke up all the other prisoners – except one, the jailer. He slept through it. I believe this is characteristic of many codependent leaders who are somehow bound inside. They have difficulty experiencing a move of God, while others seem to do so very easily. Everyone else goes home from a service or meeting with joy, but they don't. Everyone seems to be blessed by the ministry of the leader, except the leader.

The "Blessing" of an Earthquake

The jailer slept through the "revival" that was going on, but he was awakened by the earthquake that occurred (See Acts 16:25-27). The earthquake was the realization, at least as the jailer perceived it, of his worst nightmare. He thought all the prisoners had escaped. As a result, he attempted to kill himself, knowing the fate that would await him as a result of his failure at the hands of the Roman authorities. Many codependent leaders have fears of their worst nightmares catching up to them. They live with the dread of what would happen if any of their "prisoners" got out. They live under the slavery and control of the thought, "What if people found out what I really struggle with?" Like this jailer, codependent leaders fear that their "worst-case-scenario" will come to pass. Verse 27 tells us that he assumed that all the prisoners had escaped. However, *what this jailer thought was the end of his life, actually became the beginning of a new one for him.* It is possible to live free from the bondage of our false assumptions, especially those driven by the fear that we maintain about ourselves.

The Truth Shall Set You Free

Somehow knowing his intention to end his life, Paul shouted out, *"Stop, don't kill yourself. We're all here."* These words represent some very important steps needed to set every codependent leader free from their fears and false assumptions of their worst nightmares coming to pass. The truth was, this jailer's life was not to end. God was ready to provide a new beginning for him.

Sometimes, leaders are living in "prison," while holding all the keys, need to hear the truth of God's word like they never heard it before. Oh, they find it easy to tell others the Good News and the riches of living in the Kingdom of God, but they cannot ever seem to know the experience for themselves. *Fear is a distorter.* It makes us think wrongly about ourselves, others and even about God. God is not an angry Ruler in heaven waiting to strike us down at the first sign of failure. He doesn't threaten us with rejection when we fail. He doesn't become angry when we admit the struggles we battle daily. He will never be disappointed in us for admitting that we need help. No, He is not like that at all. What is God's first directive to this man, as spoken through Paul? Simply, **"Stop!"**

We must stop the codependent thinking that has predisposed us to bondage all our lives. We must stop believing distorted "truths" about others, God and ourselves. We must determine not to give in to our fears, believing that it is all over, if we admit our failings, fears and struggles. We must hear and perceive the Truth and let ourselves be set free by it.

The earthquake was a blessing in disguise. It was because of the quake that this jailer's inner bondage was exposed. As I mentioned above, it was not an end, but a new beginning. Things are never too bad to prevent God from turning our lives around. You see, the earthquake caused all the prison doors to be flung open. This includes the doors on the cells of each prisoner and the door inside the heart of this struggling leader. He asked Paul and Silas a very powerful question: *"What must I do to be saved?"* The answer: **"Believe…"**

The jailer's "wake up" call didn't come through revival; it came through the earthquake. God will use whatever He has to, in order to bring us to freedom. It is interesting how everyone was set free in the prison from the earthquake. The last person to experience freedom was the jailer.

Does this describe you? As a leader, you may have led many others to "freedom" in Christ, but are you the last one to experience what you helped others to? God's work of bringing us freedom doesn't stop until it includes YOU.

It's time to believe…again. Let the Holy Spirit guide you through the Scripture and realize that He has broken every chain of bondage through His cross. Realize that the loving and merciful God who loved us "while we were yet sinners" doesn't love you any less. He loves you now that you are His child, even with all your hang-ups. Would the One, whose goodness was intended to lead you to repentance when you didn't know Him, abandon and not be good to you now that you are His son or daughter? Never!

The next key to freedom is found in whom you should believe, namely, the **Lord Jesus**. What is the significance of this? Simply, we must realize that He is Lord and we are not. He is the One who holds and sustains all things throughout the universe, not us. *He is in control;*

therefore, we don't' have to be. Codependent leaders often act as if they are the ones responsible to keep everything together. They falsely believe that they must control everything and are driven to perform day in and day out as if the integrity and growth of the universe, the church, their family and ministry rested on their own personal successes. THEY DO NOT! They all rest on the Lord. That is what makes Him LORD.

Herein lies the lesson: God let EVERY PRISONER out of their prison cells in a way that didn't end in death. Likewise, God has a way to expose those issues that are locked up deep inside a leader that will result, not in death, but in LIFE. The first way to defeat the issues we have locked up inside us is to EXPOSE them. They must be brought into the light before we can expect them to be overcome. Fear tells us, "Keep them hidden, in the dark. If they get out, it's over for you." The truth is, if we bring them into the light, it will be a *new beginning* for us.

Like the jailer, many codependent leaders assume and bear too much responsibility. They carry emotional burdens beyond measure for any "normal" person. Calling it all "ministry" doesn't make this kind of choice a right one. In fact, it couldn't be more wrong. Believing in the Lord Jesus is an invitation to enter into His REST. The jailer could breathe easy, once everything was settled.

Leaders struggling with codependence must find the rest that God has provided for them in Christ and learn to live daily in it.

Emotionally healthy leaders are those who:

- Learn to say, "No."
- Meet other people's needs AS they meet their own (this is what "love your neighbor as yourself" means).
- Realize that their worth comes from their identity in Christ, not their performance, track record or resume. There is no room for shame in our identification with Christ.
- Learn to relinquish control as a means of getting ministry done. Instead, realize what God has called them to do, relying on the tools and people He has provided to accomplish it. Pursue excellence in completing every task as led by the Spirit of God, rather than being driven by fear. Leaders are led to success, and they lead others there as well. We should never feel *driven* to it.
- Finally, learn to have joy on the journey. Our joy is not connected to our circumstances. It is anchored in the One who never changes; the One who loves us with an everlasting love; the One who has very good plans for us and the One who is

determined to complete the good work He has begun in us through Christ.

God has called us, as leaders, to the same freedom we are leading others to experience. Don't let ministry, the pressures of the day, the opinions of others, or anything else drive you to perform in order to consider yourself a "success." *A success in the Kingdom is the one who knows the will of God and does it*. It is as simple as that. We need to be very careful not to measure success in the Kingdom by the same standards we use to measure it in the world. Remember what Jesus said about John the Baptist? "He did no miracle, yet there was no one like him on earth or in heaven that was greater." (See John 10:41 & Matthew 11:11). He built no buildings, no TV stations, no international ministry. He had nothing to show for all his labors. He ended up in jail, but he was considered by Jesus to be the "greatest."

What are the next steps for leaders struggling with codependency?

- Find someone you can be accountable to. This is someone who will tell you the truth because he or she loves you, even if you don't like hearing it.
- Develop more intimacy with God. Don't study Scripture because you need a sermon or lesson. Dig

deep into Scripture because you want to know Jesus more intimately. He will not fail to meet you in new ways.

- Begin to again regard ministry as a calling, not just a job.
- I suggest getting professional counseling. Seek out a ministry for pastors and leaders that can help you work through your codependency. There is no shame in doing so.
- The wise leader is always seeking personal development. There is no reason not to consider counseling an integral component of that development.
- Last, but certainly not least, learn to practice the "Sabbath Rest" that Jesus secured for you through His cross, resurrection and ascension. This is Kingdom living. You will do more to imitate Christ in this process than all the performance you can muster.

Let the following criteria be your barometer for "success" in ministry:

Did God show up?
Did I do what He asked me to do?

Basing your life and ministry on these two values will go far in enabling you to fulfill your calling fruitfully, which will benefit you, your family and those you are leading.

Work on renewing your mind. God has gifted and called you to lead His people. He knew that this difficult season or issue in your life would surface. He has a plan for you, and it includes resolving this for you.

Remember that it is His church. He is building it and He has the widest shoulders to bear the project: you don't! Let Him have control. He is equipped to handle it.

Be careful to avoid making the ministry your "drug of choice." Many leaders struggling with codependency make the mistake of sacrificing themselves, their spouses and their families in the name of ministry. While there are certainly sacrifices to be made in ministry, we should be careful never to sacrifice ourselves, our marriages or our families. The anointing for ministry is based on the integrity of our marriages and wholeness of our families. Our gifts will carry us only so far. We need to be sure we are forming strong bonds in our marriages and families in the course of conducting ministry. God's church is, after all, a family. Strong families make strong churches. Strong leaders build a strong family. Never let "God's Family" be the cause of the destruction of your family.

If you are working with a codependent leader:

- Pray for your leader(s). Be sure to avoid the manipulation that codependents often use to control people. Codependents usually have difficulty saying "No." Unfortunately, this predisposes them to have difficulty hearing "No" from those leading with them. However, you will do more in being a blessing to your leadership by making your Yes, yes and your No, no. There are times when "No" is the appropriate and godly answer. Don't be afraid to say it.

- Meet with your leader to discuss your core values. There are certain "non-negotiables" we need to establish in order to maintain a God-glorifying lifestyle. Sharing these with your leader will help them realize some of the boundaries they should avoid crossing or force you to cross. If there is a day in your week for family time, share this with your leader. This day must be put out of bounds for spending on ministry, unless it is a true emergency. Knowing these boundaries in advance will go far to help everyone know what to expect from each other and maintain productive and peaceful partnerships.

- Discuss a list of priorities with your leader. One thing that helps to keep me balanced in my ministry is to think on what I would tell someone from the congregation who came to me with the dilemma I am facing. What would I advise them to do? For example, if I suggested a priority list for them to achieve balance in their lives, it might look like the following:

- o My relationship with God is first;
- o My relationship with my spouse is second;
- o My relationship with my family is third;
- o My job is fourth (ministry goes here);
- o A list of priorities that will work for a congregant, must also work for a leader. We must be sure we duplicate the right model for the people we lead. Whether it is the right one or the wrong one, the model we live will certainly be duplicated, so be careful. A healthy or unhealthy leader reproduces "after his/her kind" throughout the congregation.

When discussing these matters with a leader, do so in private. If necessary, bring another leader with you for additional follow-up discussions. Speak the truth in love and believe God to help promote unity between all involved. After all, it is where unity prevails that God commands the blessing.

Profile Three: A Rich, Young Ruler

How A Performance Mindset And An Addiction To Approval Undermines Our Potential To Fulfill Our Destiny

Key Scripture: Mark 10:17-31

Rich, young and having authority: who could ask for anything more? Surely this is a recipe for success in anyone's book. Most young people have zeal and energy, but little money and authority. Once we get old enough to have authority through years of experience, we may not have much money left, especially after raising a family, paying tuitions and planning to have something left for retirement. As far as ruling is concerned, our scope of authority may only extend to our immediate family, our job or other areas in which we serve. Not so with our young friend in Mark's Gospel. He had it all: the energy of youth, the finances to accomplish something and the authority to make an impact with them. By all measures, in our contemporary culture, he would be called a "success."

Let me ask you a question, "What does a successful church leader look like?" Before you answer too quickly, be sure to think carefully about it. Think about what standards you would use to measure success. Would the measures you use be applicable in all cultures around the world? Would they be applicable in every epoch of history? Would they be applicable for all leaders in the ministry, regardless of race, ethnicity, economics, political position or the assets available? Would they be solidly based on Biblical measures of success or worldly ones? Perhaps this is not such an easy question to answer after all.

Is Anyone Truly "Good"?

This young ruler came running up to Jesus and addressed Him as Good Teacher. Jesus responded to him in an unusual way. He didn't say, *"Yes, how can I help you?"* He didn't even answer his question at first. No, the first thing Jesus said sounded like He was challenging the young man. *"Why do you call me good?"* Jesus said, *"Only God is truly good."* It was almost as if Jesus knew what was going on inside the mind of this young leader. We know that Jesus never wasted words. If He made a statement prior to answering a question, there had to be a good reason for it. I believe Jesus did have a very good reason to make the statement. He was challenging what this man must have considered a core belief of his. I suggest that it may have been the notion that *good people inherit eternal life.*

When we examine the statement of Jesus and His use of the word "good" as translated in New Testament Greek, we understand that word to mean someone who is *intrinsically* good. According to that definition, Jesus was correct in stating that only God was intrinsically good. I suppose we can surmise that Jesus was stating that since only God is intrinsically good, this young man calling Jesus good was an inference that he thought Jesus was God. That may be, but I believe Jesus had another reason. Jesus was challenging what the young ruler apparently believed about himself. Since God was only truly intrinsically good, on what basis did this young man imply his own goodness? I believe there is only one answer. It was his performance.

This man ran up to Jesus, but he actually ran into Him. Proceeding to answer his question, Jesus began with, *"you know the commandments..."* and then enumerated the ones that appeared on the second tablet of the law. These were the commandments pertaining to how we relate to our neighbor. The first tablet lists the commandments for how we relate to God. I suspect that this young ruler thought he knew the answer to his question and was confident that Jesus would agree with him. However, the end of the story depicts him walking away from Jesus, face fallen and filled with sadness. What happened? This young man was bound by a belief that eternal life was earned by being good, doing good works and obeying the commandments. The level of sadness with which he left Jesus is a clue to us as to how much he expected to be approved by Him. However, things did not work out as he had expected.

There are leaders in the body of Christ who struggle with the same problem as this young ruler. They think that God's approval of them rests upon their own efforts and good works. They are hardworking, right living people; obeying the rules. They maintain a high quality, moral lifestyle in their efforts to please God and other people. However, they experience repeated disappointment when things don't work out as they first expected. This rich, young ruler was bound by what we will call a *performance trap*. People trapped in this way of thinking carry their resumes with them everywhere they go. They always feel compelled to do the right thing in every circumstance. They crave – and desperately need – approval, which make them feel like they have accomplished something. This will confirm that they are making progress. This will represent a rewarding experience for them. At this point, you may be thinking, *"Ok, so what's the problem?"* The problem is that, to people like this young leader, approval makes them feel good about themselves. Without it, they disapprove of themselves and fear that others will as well. When we find ourselves running up to Jesus (or significant others in our lives) with our resumes in hand, anticipating approval, we may instead be disappointed by the response. We just might walk away from that encounter very sorrowful.

Addicted to Approval

How does an addiction to approval start in a person's life? It begins, as most dysfunctions do, with a belief system. Those beliefs give rise to a mindset. A mindset gives rise to our basic emotional baseline. Our basic emotional baseline gives rise to our behavior. Those behaviors, lived out consistently over time, produce a lifestyle. Approval addicts bound in a performance trap usually maintain a belief that sounds like some form of the following statement:

"I must have the approval of certain other people in order to feel good about myself."

For the approval addict, self-concept is not based as much upon how we view ourselves, but on our perception of how others view us. Like this young man, we work very hard on being good. We do the right things, go to the right places and connect with the right people. We base our lives on the way we think others perceive us, causing us to become addicted to their approval. There are traces of codependency in this type of person. They usually cannot say, "No." In fact, they are usually overly compliant and go far beyond the call of duty in doing what people ask of them. They are always available. They carry too many responsibilities and seem to be able to accomplish all of them, but not without a considerable cost to themselves and others. While on the surface they seem like "self-sacrificing saints" in actuality, they aren't. They work. They are driven. These people are high achievers. There is nothing necessarily wrong with being a high achiever. We just need to ask the question, *"Why?"* The issue is not so much about *what* one is doing, but *why* he or she is doing so much of it. Perhaps the following story will help clarify what I mean:

> A very successful businessman walked into the office of a Christian University President and sat down. They were friends and knew each other on a first name basis. The businessman was the CEO of his company and lived a lifestyle one would expect of a person with his acumen for business. The man looked disturbed, and the President of the University asked him, *"What's wrong, Tom?"* He answered, **"Howard, I've spent my life climbing the ladder of success, only after reaching the top, to discover that it was leaning against the wrong wall."**

Let me explain:

You see, this man realized that his expectations of what he thought would bring him a sense of fulfillment and meaning, resulted in bringing none. Instead, while there were many other results of his efforts that he enjoyed, they weren't the ones he needed and desired.

Blessing or Problem?

Leaders must be very discerning when it comes to developing other leaders. When an overworked pastor sees an up-and-coming young person who seems to have leadership ability, they light up. When they notice how many activities they are involved with in at the church, they often say, *"I wish I had ten more people like you."* While this sounds like an encouragement to someone who could be a great asset to the team, it may indicate a potentially serious problem. Approval addicts often don't finish strong. Instead, they usually burn out over time. Either they do this as a result of overwork, or they implode because they haven't received the approval, recognition or promotion they anticipated and just quit altogether. In my experience of pastoring for twenty-five years (21 of them as a Senior Pastor), I have seen many hard-working servants of God doing all they can to please the Lord in ministry. Whenever I saw someone involved in several ministries of the church, it represented a possible red flag to me. Rather than assign another responsibility to that person, even though they asked for it, I would ask some questions first. If they were married, I would ask how their spouse was doing? How was your marriage doing? If they had children, I would ask, *"How are your kids? How much time do you usually spend with them?"* If they were single, I would ask them if they had any friends. *"Are you engaged in meaningful relationships with other groups of people outside of church?"* Finally, I would ask if they had any hobbies or practiced any recreational activities. I would conduct this "interview" in an attempt to rescue a potential approval addict from a destructive end. The ministry always needs workers. However, no ministry needs to be staffed by an approval addict.

What drives the approval addict? There are two forces that drive an addiction to approval. They both involve fear. The first is a fear of rejection. The second is a fear of failure. Approval addicts are usually perfectionistic. They strive to do everything well which, in itself, is fine. However, striving to do so out of a fear of failure or rejection to the level of being perfectionistic is unhealthy and destructive. We must remember Paul's word to his protégé, Timothy, a young man with leadership potential. Paul said, *"God has not given us the spirit of fear, but of love, power and a sound (disciplined) mind." (2 Tim. 1:7).*

Performance is not the criteria Jesus uses to raise up a leader. While a good leader must possess certain gifts and qualities of leadership, performance driven by fear is not something Jesus approves of. Perfectionism, driven by fear, may make a person seem like they have leadership potential, but this may only be an external veneer. Under that exterior may be a frustrated and, possibly, depressed person who just cannot understand why he or she is constantly being taken advantage of by others. They long for the time when they will finally receive the recognition they believe they deserve, but usually never comes.

Leaders who are driven by the approval of others fall into a snare that enslaves them. They say things like, *"We must maintain a high standard of performance and encourage others to do so as well."* They are present at every meeting; are involved in every activity in the church and, to some degree, neglect themselves and/or their families for the sake of the ministry. They do this because they believe that, if they don't, everything will begin falling apart. The fact is, other people won't model your performance at a perfectionistic level. Most people realize that this is not emotionally or physically healthy.

Often, when staff or team members don't follow the leader's example, the leader doubles down and begins to enforce more rules and regulations on others. This is where the element of control comes into play. Leaders who are approval addicts use the threat of rejection or giving recognition and approval, to promote and reward the desired behavior in others. This is highly manipulative. Such practices can easily become the culture of the ministry, the family or the organization. When it does, it serves to have the exact opposite effect. People either leave or they don't get involved. Self-deception can come into play at this point as well. The leader often mistakenly concludes, *"The devil is attacking the church,"* when, in fact, they are destroying it by their own hand.

When Jesus Sticks His Finger Where It Hurts

The next significant statement Jesus made to this young man sounded like this could have been everything he was waiting to hear. Jesus said, *"You lack only one thing..."* Can you imagine how his heart must have been pounding when he heard this? Would he finally hear someone give him the recognition he deserved? Could this be the "pay day" that he had been striving for all his life up to this point? I am certain his expectations and his hopes were sky high. But then…the one thing Jesus cited as yet to be done was, *"Sell all your possessions and give the money to the poor and you will have treasure in heaven. Then come and follow me." (Matthew 19:21).*

How could Jesus say this? Didn't He know what a blow this would be to this man? Did He have any idea of how hard this would hit him? I am certain He knew all these things. However, we must realize that Jesus was after something; some 'one thing' He needed to help this man be rid of. It was his addiction to approval. You see, when Jesus instructed him to sell all his possessions, he was asking the man to empty his "trophy case" and burn all the symbols of his success. Jesus knew that he was a slave to his possessions. He didn't possess them; they possessed him.

Jesus will often stick His finger where it hurts, because that is the one place where He knows we need healing and freedom. This man interpreted all he had amassed throughout his life as evidence of how good he was. I am sure he learned, through experience, that this was the basis on which he earned the acceptance of others. To him, this was a "successful" formula. But this time, in Jesus' eyes, it was working against him. This young ruler was confronted with two powerful truths. First, success in the Kingdom is not measured the way it is measured in the world. Jesus doesn't approve of us based upon our works, abilities or accomplishments. Our acceptance by Jesus is based solely on His great love for us. Secondly, in order to follow Jesus, we must place Him first above all other trophies and priorities in our lives. Jesus doesn't want anything to occupy center stage in our hearts but Him.

Love Hurts When It Aims to Heal

The most important part of verse 21 is this: *"Looking at the man, Jesus felt genuine love for him."* This preceded His next statement regarding the "one thing." He LOVED him. That may sound strange, but it isn't. Love is the motivation in EVERYTHING Jesus does. Jesus not only knew this would cause the man to become sorrowful, but He also knew he would walk away. Do you see how significant the resolution of this issue is for Jesus regarding the heart of a leader? Love let the young man walk. Love let him choose.

Any one of us may have stopped and pleaded with the man to reconsider. We would have tried to explain what we meant by what we said. We might even be tempted to water down what we said in an effort not to lose such a great leadership candidate. We might have, but Jesus didn't. Jesus didn't want the man's possessions. He wanted the man's heart. He knew it was held captive, not by possessions, but by the faulty thinking that drove the man's performance. If he didn't become free from his "addiction," the weight of ministry would eventually crush him.

God's Unconditional Acceptance

The fundamental truth that we must realize if we are to lead others in the Body of Christ is that God fully and unconditionally accepts us through our Lord Jesus Christ (See Colossians 1:22). Because we are unconditionally loved and accepted by our Father, through Christ, we don't *need* the acceptance of certain other people in order to feel good about ourselves. Once we reject this false belief, we will be able to embark on the road to freedom and lead others there. Our belief will change to become, "I would *like* the approval of certain other people, but I don't *need* it any longer."

This realization will revolutionize our ability to lead successfully. No longer will we be manipulated by the opinions of other people. No longer will we fear rejection by others. When we know we are unconditionally accepted by God and are doing what He has commanded us to do, our thoughts will change, our emotions will change and our lifestyles will change. No longer will we need to fear failure, because it has now become a learning opportunity, rather than a reason for rejection. In short, we will now be able to live knowing that we are loved for *who we are* and not by what we do.

Damian Smeragliuolo

Everything is Possible With God

Jesus closed the lesson to the disciples with this statement, *"Everything is possible with God."* You see, it is not difficult for rich people to enter the Kingdom of Heaven because of their riches. It is difficult for them to enter because riches, as emblems of our success and the basis for our acceptance, expose a heart with divided loyalties. We simply cannot serve two masters. Jesus said it would be impossible. We must have one loyalty: one reason for being. The Bible calls this a pure, or undivided heart. When the only thing that "possesses" us is that we are captivated by the love of God in Christ and live for Him *because we have His approval*, we can live and lead in a freedom like we have never known before.

Leading others from a position of freedom will create a culture of freedom within any organization, especially a church. Like Jesus, leaders will meet people where they are and encourage, not force, them to "come up higher." They let people develop at their own pace and to their own realistic potential. Some grow thirty, others sixty and still others to a hundred-fold increase. This is the surest path to maturity on an individual and corporate level. This is the way the body of Christ becomes engaged in the Kingdom process of edifying itself in love. Love lets people walk, and it also lets people grow.

Personal Testimony

I was raised by a very strict, demanding father. Although I worked in the family business since early childhood, my father was a man that would rarely recognize or reward good behavior. If he did recognize my good work, he expressed it through my mother, rather than speak directly to me. I grew up learning to work hard. Once I asked for a raise, I was told to put in more hours at night. Reinforcement was rarely given for my efforts, then I learned to work harder and harder, all in the hopeful expectation that recognition would come. However, I never knew when, or if, it would come.

I was an excellent student. I never got into trouble as a teenager or young adult and always strove to do the right thing. I learned to be compliant, constantly expecting that approval would come. I was a lot like the rich young ruler. I couldn't think of being different in any way. I kept pushing along, working harder, expecting approval from professors in college, managers at work, friends, anyone. I believed that I needed the approval of others in order to feel good about myself. Even when I became a born-again Christian, I vowed that I would be the best son to my heavenly Father that I could be. I am sure you can begin to understand what it took me years to discover: I was addicted to approval.

Once I learned that I was fully and completely accepted by my heavenly Father, I was set free. I can testify that I am living in the freedom of being a son, accepted by the Father, doing what He has called me to do – regardless of what others think. The positive or negative opinions of others don't drive my behavior any longer. This has resulted in enabling me to focus on what God, not people, expects of me. I learned to say, "No." This has resulted in an inner peace and confidence that has led to a sense of purpose and satisfaction that keeps me on a steady path to finish my course and fulfill my destiny in God's plan for my life. I encourage you to take whatever steps are necessary to get set free from the addiction to approval. Discover and fulfill your destiny in God's plan for your life.

Next Steps:

If you are a leader struggling with an addiction to approval:

- Realize that you cannot be driven by fear of failure or rejection. You may need to reflect on where these two fears may have taken root in your life. It may be necessary to seek professional counseling in the process of doing so;

- Seek the counsel of another leader outside your church or organization. If you can be candid and transparent with them on this subject, do so. You will gain by the objectivity they may be able to offer you. **Warning:** don't seek the counsel of a leader who is "wired" the same way you are. This is not a time to receive affirmation as a way of avoiding necessary steps to make some significant changes in your life;

- Give yourself and others the freedom to fail. It is often our failures that make the best "teachers." Examine each failure (yours and theirs), asking, *"What can we learn from this,"* or *"What do we think God is trying to teach us through this experience?"*

- Remember, a church, where love is the key, should be the safest place in which to fail and work on getting it right. Let us be sure not to create the exact opposite environment by being driven by perfectionism and driving others by the same.

- Realize that we are completely accepted by the Father through Christ by faith, not our performance. When we really begin to believe that, we will find a new freedom that will result in us desiring to have the approval of others, but no longer *needing* it;

- Work on consistently building up staff based on who they are, rather than by their performance. This is not as easy as it seems. Often in our acknowledgement of our appreciation of staff, we cite performance. We must be careful to reward personal characteristics and gifts, not just productivity. When we appreciate people for who they are, we will be on our way to building a closely-knit family who will sacrifice for the benefit of the whole. Without this, staff will look at their position as "just a job" until they find another one more pleasing or personally rewarding to them;

- Avoid the temptation to be the "face" of everything that goes on in your church or area of ministry. When you feel the temptation to "take center stage" ask yourself, *"Why?"* Ask, *"What difference will my input make beyond what has already been said or done?"* Give others a chance to share the success in public. Your coworkers will appreciate it, and the congregation, or department, will know that you are being selfless in an effort to let others shine. This will elevate you in the eyes of those you lead.

If your leader is an approval addict:

- A leader who is addicted (emphasis on ADDICTED) to approval can be very challenging to work with. Usually, they will see your performance as a direct commentary on them, and not you. In other words, they perceive your success and approval by others as approval of them and their leadership. This can become a secondary "addiction." The opposite is also true. When you fail, they feel like they have failed. This may result in micro-managing or being overbearing to staff. The micro-managing may be masked under the guise of seeking excellence. However, while we all want to do our best, this extreme striving for "excellence" is an excuse for more control, which stifles growth and development of other leaders;

- Leadership development can be challenging as well. This type of leader will find it difficult for team members to excel in their gift and calling, especially if they "outshine" the leader (in the leader's own eyes, that is). This leader has an inordinate need to appear to be the expert in everything;

- To function effectively in this kind of environment, you must find ways to incorporate the leader's input as integral to your success. I am not endorsing being deceptive in any way or false. However, you will never want to place yourself in a competitive or adversarial position with the leadership. This is not a good situation to be in. If the leader is also very insecure, you may want to prayerfully consider another place to serve. The issue here is to *"be wise as a serpent, but harmless as a dove."* (See Matthew 10:16). For example, you may want to include the leader in team meetings for specific projects to elicit their input and suggestions. Whether all their suggestions are implemented or not, the key is that you got them involved. Therefore, they have a share in your success. In the business world, this is called, "managing upward;"

- It would be wise to speak of and celebrate your successes as a "team effort" that wouldn't have been possible without everyone's input. Unfortunately, the success of another, without the input of the leader, may make the leader feel "threatened," and they may begin to treat you as an antagonist. This will make the leader feel that they have "license" to be more controlling, provide less autonomy and offer little empowerment, if any at all;

- Model forgiveness and restoration with your own teammates who fail. Demonstrate the process of analyzing the problem, discern what went wrong, plan for a strategy to avoid a repetition of the failure and release the teammate to try again.

Profile Four: Joseph

Overcoming Disappointments While

Keeping Your Dreams Alive

Key Scripture: Genesis 37-50

The story of Joseph in the Old Testament is a story of extremes. Having been born to Jacob in his old age, Joseph became his favorite. His father gave him a coat of many colors, singling him out from the rest of his brothers. Not only did his father single him out, but God singled him out as well. Joseph had a dream. He shared this dream with his brothers and his parents. He saw himself as a sheaf of wheat in the field: it was the largest one and all the other sheaves bowed down to it. He also saw himself as a celestial body that the sun, moon and eleven other stars gave homage to. When he shared his dreams with his brothers, they became extremely jealous of him and could not speak a kind word to him. Even his parents questioned whether they too would give homage to their youngest son. This was a far-fetched prospect indeed, especially in a patriarchal, Middle Eastern culture. While Jacob didn't understand the meaning of Joseph's dreams, he wondered what they could possibly have meant.

From that point on, Joseph's story is a series of one disappointment after another. These were not minor disappointments, but very traumatic ones, each seemingly worse than the one before it. How did he survive? How did he cope? How was he able to hang on for so long? How could it be that all these experiences didn't result in Joseph being in therapy all his life? Any one of them…give up, call it quits, harden heart and settle…unforgiveness; but that didn't happen. What enabled him to press forward?

The answers to these questions are bound up in a single statement of Joseph's, which he spoke at the end of his dramatic story. His is the story of a man who started well and ended well. All that occurred in between revealed a process of how the attributes and character of a person are forged. They carried him to the finish line. After being reunited with his brothers and family and after all they had put him through, he stated, *"You meant it for evil, but God meant it for good."* But how did Joseph get there?

We won't delve into each incident in his life in great depth. For our purposes, I will discuss how Joseph responded to major times of crisis in his life and overcame them.

Joseph was a person just like the rest of us. He lived in a family much like our own. There were dysfunctions in his family: he was hated by his brothers, favored by his father and even his brothers' attempt to murder him was thwarted by another brother. It wasn't easy to be a member of his family. In fact, it was because he came from such a dysfunctional family that the rest of his problems occurred. He was the victim of a "staged killing" perpetrated by his brothers. He was sold into slavery, framed for a crime he didn't commit and forgotten in jail for two years as a result of a broken promise. Finally, he was released from prison and promoted to the position of Prime Minister of a nation. You just can't make this stuff up!

Can you identify with any aspect of Joseph's experiences? I am sure there may be one or two items we can identify with. Perhaps some of us can identify with more. Still others may have even worse experiences we could add to the list. Regardless of how you may identify with Joseph, there is one major fact we can point to as the moral of his story: it is simply that:

> *You can come from a severely dysfunctional family and have been victimized by circumstances beyond your control for most of your life, but that doesn't mean you cannot finish well and fulfill your destiny in the plan of God.*

How Joseph responded to each of the incidents he faced serves as examples to every leader on how to respond to setbacks, especially those that are beyond your control. Joseph didn't start out as a leader, but he finished as one. This indicates to me that *leaders are not born: they are made.* Let us follow his climb to victory.

The Power of a Dream

What do you dream about? Where do you see yourself in five, ten or fifteen years? I am not asking about any far-fetched fantasy, but I am asking about what your realistic imaginations are of what you want to become. These are imaginations that are within the realm of the possible, but far enough out of reach to require personal development and Divine intervention to cause them to become reality.

Dreams are powerful. There are some dreams that come from God Himself. He has placed desires, capabilities, abilities and potential into every one of us. Those desires become expressed in us as dreams or imaginations of things we see ourselves achieving. I realize Joseph never thought he would become the Prime Minister of Egypt, but he certainly had a sense of destiny about his life. Do you have any dreams? Do you see yourself accomplishing any form of success that will be satisfying and fulfilling to you? Dreams are important. They have the power to sustain us when everything else going on in our lives seems to point to their impossibility. A dream is what makes us try again, start over, endure and fight through obstacles until we reach our goals. However, dreams can become problematic, especially when you share them with your brothers.

If I could ask Joseph what he would do differently, if he could, he would probably say, *"I shouldn't have shared my dreams with my brothers. They weren't ready for them."* There is wisdom in that, and it leads us to the first of six lessons we can learn from the life of Joseph.

Lesson One: You cannot share your dreams with others who have no dreams of their own.

When you come from a dysfunctional family, although you may assume that they would be among your best supporters, they may, in fact, not be. Jealousy, pessimism, envy and even hatred can flow in a dysfunctional family. When people feel stuck, deprived of opportunities and short-changed in their lives, it is very difficult to be happy and celebrate another family member's dreams. *This is not a reason to never express your dreams, but to be very selective in how you do so, when you do and to whom you share them.* If Joseph had limited his revelation to his parents, perhaps he would not have been sold into slavery. In an emotionally healthy family, everyone should rejoice in the dreams for success held by any other member of the family. This should be the case in church families and other organizational groups as well.

Let's face it: there are dysfunctional churches and other organizations just like there are dysfunctional families.

When emotionally unhealthy leaders or team members are in charge, it is very difficult for a person to rise up and speak of overcoming and achieving success. There is often an attitude and an atmosphere of arrogance in the organization. Others may say things like, *"You haven't paid your dues yet,"* or *"We've been laboring here for decades; do you think you're going to come in now and change things?"* I think you get the picture. Suffice to say, be selective in sharing your dreams and visions. Share them with someone who is a mature, godly leader and won't feel threatened or undermined by your revelation. On the contrary, they will celebrate with you and spur you on to achieve these dreams and visions in order to fulfill your destiny. Every emotionally healthy leader and church family should be eager to see young leaders excel and out-succeed them, doing all they can to assist them in the process.

Lesson Two: Live your core values.

What are your core values? What are those "non-negotiables" that you will not compromise, but choose to live by them consistently? Core values are the standards you live by that circumstances cannot force you to abandon or modify.

His own brothers sold Joseph as a slave. He served in the house of a man named Potiphar. He was pulled from hearth and home and placed into slavery. He wore an iron collar. He went from wearing a coat of many colors to an iron collar. Who could psychologically survive that, not to mention physically? But Joseph did. How? He knew how to *not allow the chains on the outside to cause him to become chained on the inside.* His inner values, the person he was, his character and integrity, were not dependent upon outward circumstances. As a result, although a prisoner on the outside, he was able to live as a free man on the inside. He was free to be the person he truly was.

Joseph was successful in all he did in Potiphar's house. The Bible tells us that God was with Joseph and everything Joseph did was done with excellence, gaining him favor with Potiphar. In fact, Potiphar eventually gave Joseph the responsibility of his entire household as Chief Steward. Oh, we could certainly justify Joseph, if he approached his responsibilities as a slave with resentment. Who could blame him? However, Joseph apparently knew the secret about maintaining his inner, core values. He knew that he had to respond, not react, to his circumstances in a way that *enabled him to remain bless-able in the sight of God.*

Many people fail to experience this when forced to do something they don't like doing. What do I mean by forced? Well, let us take a person who is called to be a pastor. He joins a new church and is asked to teach a children's Sunday School class, usher or (heaven forbid) help the church janitorial staff. When approaching these tasks with resentment or anger because he feels he is *above* them, he places himself in a position where God cannot bless him. Joseph realized that he could not allow his present circumstances to have an impact on the Divine dreams that God gave him. Because of this, God caused Potiphar's entire household to be blessed and prosper. The Bible informs us that *"promotion comes from the Lord."* (See Psalm 75:6-7). When we live in a way that makes us bless-able before God, He makes sure that we obtain favor and will promote us in due time. In addition, God will cause the whole organization to be blessed and prosper, because one person lives out his core values.

Lesson Three: Being Seduction-Proof.

We live in a promiscuous culture where everything and anything goes. Scandals abound. It seems that not a day goes by where we don't hear of someone's life being destroyed by money, sex or fame. In fact, our culture seems to reward those who are "smart" enough to "play the game" to get ahead in this world, even if that game involves something illegal or immoral. Our amoral culture considers those who commit illegal acts as "smart," as long as you don't get caught. We live in a culture where the ends justify the means. Values, character and integrity, if they are mentioned at all, are considered weaknesses rather than the strengths they are.

Joseph was a handsome guy. He was smart, talented and his "star was rising" in Egypt. In our success-crazed culture, a person like Joseph would be attractive to everyone at every level of society. Potiphar's wife became attracted to him. She tried to seduce him to sleep with her. As a matter of fact, she harangued him daily, trying to get him to do so. Finally, he ran out of the palace to escape her clutches, leaving his outer garment in her hand. Angered by this, she framed him and accused him of attempting to assault her. Needless to say, Potiphar didn't take this lightly and threw him in jail.

This experience in Joseph's life begs the question: *"What price are you willing to pay to maintain your integrity before God?"* Let's face it; there are a multitude of opportunities we are exposed to in our lives that threaten to seduce us into compromising our values and integrity. What stops us from engaging them? What causes us to see them as evil or sinful, rather than opportunities to advance our careers and gain favor from the inside? How can we remain seduction-proof?

The first step in remaining seduction-proof is to have in advance, before the situation arises, made a decision about certain things you will never compromise. We need to adopt the conviction that there are issues that are black or white, right or wrong and sinful or righteous. In our increasingly "gray" and amoral world, it is time for us to take a stand for what God values, over what the world around us values. In the case of a leader, this is a very serious core value. We need to ask and answer the question in advance, *"Are we willing to pay the price of doing right, even if it lands us in jail?"*

I witnessed a sad and incriminating example of this while watching TV recently. The staff of some gossip show was criticizing a young pro-football player. In fact, they were ridiculing him. Why? He admitted that he was a virgin. They spoke of him as if he were some kind of freak. What has happened to our society? He has strong core values and has chosen to live by them. He was willing to endure the criticism of others, rather than compromise.

Leaders must have the conviction of what is right and wrong. Every leader must decide, in advance, what is in and out of bounds. *Our boundary lines cannot be drawn by cultural standards, but by God's standards.* When a leader develops this conviction, he or she may have to pay a price for maintaining it. However, the price of maintaining it far outweighs the price of succumbing to the seduction. Imagine if Joseph gave in to the temptation posed by Potiphar's wife. He would have forfeited the office of Prime Minister of Egypt. God would not and could not have blessed him with advancement if he had. To be seduction-proof, a leader must always live by God's standards of right and wrong. When we do, and pay the price for it, God's hands are still free to bless us. He will even reverse a jail sentence if He must.

Lesson Four: Bloom where you land.

When Joseph landed in jail as a result of being framed by Potiphar's wife, a very interesting thing happened. Would you believe that the Lord was with Joseph and he gained the favor of the prison warden? The warden even put Joseph in charge of the entire prison. The Bible tells us in Genesis 39:3 that *the Lord was with him and caused everything he did to succeed.* Here is just another example of Joseph remaining bless-able before God. Joseph's core values, integrity and standard of life were still at work in him IN PRISON. Don't misunderstand; prison life was no picnic. However, when God's blessing is upon you,

"...He makes even your enemies be at peace with you."
(See Proverbs 16:7).

Joseph still had his gifts, talents, abilities and capacities. Remarkably, he didn't let his circumstances stop him from using them. He even interpreted the dreams of two inmates. The interpretations he gave them came true. God gave Joseph the interpretation that the chief cupbearer would be restored to his position in three days. It happened just as he said it would.

What do you think would have happened if Joseph had become bitter at the way he was falsely accused and jailed? He could have sulked all day long for each day he was imprisoned. He could have complained about how unfair the system was and how all the good he had done in Potiphar's house was easily forgotten. However, *because of his intense loyalty to God, he used his gifts and abilities in every situation he found himself, despite the circumstances.* Remarkably, the cupbearer remembered Joseph after two years on an occasion when the king had a dream and sought an interpretation (See Genesis 41). The cupbearer remembered Joseph and recommended him to interpret the king's dream. Joseph's interpretation was used by God to save the nation during a famine, and Joseph was promoted to Prime Minister. Here is the point: Joseph bloomed where he landed by using his gifts, and

God used his gifts for what God knew was coming. The result was advancement and promotion!

An emotionally healthy leader blooms where he lands. He must believe that God knows that days of hardship, wrongful accusations and prison would come. However, God also knows that the shortest distance between Joseph becoming the Chief Steward and the Prime Minister was a two-year jail sentence. When a leader blooms where he lands, he demonstrates a faith that says, *"God is in complete control of my life."* God will never fail such a leader.

Lesson Five: Maintain a heart for restoration.

In Genesis 42, we see an elaborate plan executed by Joseph that seems out of character for him. His brothers travel to Egypt because they heard that there was food there during the famine. They don't recognize him at first, thinking he was an Egyptian. Joseph puts them in prison, subsequently releases them and puts their payment for the grain they purchased back in their sacks. He sends them with instructions to return with their youngest brother and father. They all eventually return, and Joseph finally reveals himself to them all. This is probably one of the most moving and dramatic events in Biblical history.

Here is the lesson: all leaders will experience hurt from time to time and some will be more intense than others. The most painful ones may even come from some other "family" member, someone we trusted, loved and gave of ourselves for their good. You see, we usually are at risk to be hurt the most by the ones to whom we make ourselves most vulnerable. That means "family" will sometimes be the source of our greatest pain. An emotionally healthy leader will never seek revenge. He will never want to see others pay the price for their sins against him. An emotionally healthy leader will always strive to maintain a tender heart of restoration with his brothers. This is of major importance in the life of a leader. *When we act in a loving and compassionate way to those who hurt us, we are acting most like God.* It is not that we excuse the wrong that was done to us. Instead, we forgive it. Having a heart of compassion, predisposed to forgiveness and reconciliation, will result in God's blessing of restoration. He will do this for a person, a family and a nation.

Lesson Six: Having a Heaven-oriented perspective about everything.

I wish I could produce a movie that could fully capture the scene of Joseph identifying himself to his brothers and weeping with them in loving reconciliation (See Genesis 45). When confronting them, he stated further, *"Don't be* *upset and don't be angry with yourselves for selling me to this place. **It was God who sent me here ahead of you to preserve your lives.***"

Wow! What an outlook on his life that Joseph demonstrates for us here. Joseph's worldview (and his life-view) was that he saw the hand of God in everything that happened to him. This is one of the foremost qualities that a good, emotionally healthy leader must possess. This is not to say that God caused everything to happen to Joseph, but that He allowed it to happen.

The realization that God *"works everything together for the good of those who love Him and are called according to His purposes"* (Romans 8:28) can never be defeated. This attitude eliminates so much guilt, pain and shame from being felt by the entire family. This mindset was foundational to Joseph's entire life. When an emotionally healthy leader has an attitude like this, every situation becomes a win-win for the leader and everyone else in the family. This is true in a biological family and an organizational one.

When we allow bitterness, resentment and anger, even at God, to fester in our lives, it threatens to pollute our entire being, our families and the church. Not only that, but it ties God's hands from moving on our behalf. Imagine what could happen if we never allowed short-term pains to blind us to long-term gains? Lives would be transformed on a wholesale level. *When we allow God to reveal His perspective to us in every situation, He imparts LIFE to all involved.*

There is so much more that can be said about Joseph and all that God did through him and for him. I have chosen to present these fundamental thoughts about his life to you because I believe them to be his core values. They will help create an atmosphere of healing and restoration that will impact the culture of a family, organization and nation. They will foster the development of emotionally healthy leaders and followers. *Joseph's story is of a leader who was made, not born.* He is a model leader that has learned how to turn the most painful circumstances into opportunities for growth. Emotionally healthy leaders seize opportunities to do this consistently, modeling, cultivating and duplicating these values in those who follow them.

Profile Five: King Saul

Insecurity And The Snare Of Searching For Identity In What We Do

Key Scripture: 1 Samuel 9-11

Growing up in the United States, I have always heard our country described as "The Land of Opportunity." To a great extent, I believe this to be true. Certainly, thousands of people have come from other countries and found opportunities here that have transformed their lives. The story of Israel's first king is the story of a man who was given many opportunities, perhaps as no other man or leader had been given. However, it is also a story of how many of them were missed or abused by him. You see, just because an opportunity to lead comes our way, it doesn't necessarily mean we will be able to seize or sustain it automatically and succeed.

One of the most fundamental characteristics and quality that a good leader must have is a sound sense of security. A leader must be confident in *who they are,* in addition to what they know. Unfortunately, many leaders who know very much often fail as a direct result of insecurity and not knowing who they are. When a leader or any person, for that matter, know who they are, they are enabled to develop a strong sense of identity. A strong identity enables a leader to lead in accordance with their gifts, knowledge and abilities, with a confidence that will help stabilize them personally, the organizations they lead and, more importantly, the people in those organizations. Regardless of what level of leadership you find yourself, a sound sense of security and identity will empower you to lead successfully and develop and empower other leaders working together with you.

Insecurity, often coupled with low esteem, isn't readily evident in a leader. In fact, there are leaders who are considered successful that have risen to the top of their field who battle insecurity and low esteem daily. Often, the pain resulting from this is what drives some leaders. Being driven may result in accomplishing things and getting promoted - the *marks of success*. However, insecurity and low esteem undermine that leader on a personal level. The pressures of success often prove too heavy for a person with such a weak internal foundation, often resulting in some level of collapse. That collapse comes in the form of physical and emotional breakdown, moral failure, addictions, failed marriages, fragmented families, limited or no growth and, ultimately, failed organizations.

In this Profile, we will trace the progression of how, because of insecurity, Saul *set himself up* for failure and discuss what remedies he could have employed to prevent it. Saul's experience in leadership is a classic example of the violation of two cardinal rules for leaders. First, never let the circumstances drive you into a potentially destructive or bad decision. Secondly, never let your emotions drive you into a potentially destructive or bad decision. While we all struggle with some degree of insecurity, Saul's story is one where the struggle was the central, underlying force of his entire life.

Don't Judge a Book By Its Cover

We live in an image-driven culture. Marketing experts are paid millions of dollars to present products to consumers every day in ways that will appeal to them and get them to make a purchase. It is all about the packaging, the presentation, the optics, and almost never about actual substance. There is a car commercial running at the time of this writing that exemplifies this trend. The emotion of LOVE is associated with families and individuals appearing in the commercial. Touching scenes of various sorts are shown, each eliciting a strong emotional response from viewers. The tag line at the end is *"Love, that's what makes a (car brand) ..."* what it is. We don't hear about mileage, safety, durability, resale value, mechanical soundness or performance. After all, aren't those the items on anyone's checklist who is shopping for a car?

Even though we know this, we are still moved by the packaging, the label or the emotion so skillfully attached to the visuals. Ours is a culture of *branding.* Everywhere we look: on billboards, storefronts, T-shirts and even tattoos, we see brands that enable us to immediately identify products, people, ideas and movements. While there are many instances I can cite, a phrase illustrates my point very clearly. I heard it used by a news commentator in a recent Presidential election. It was the phrase, *"He looks very presidential."* What does that even mean? Would that phrase mean the same thing in every other nation in the world? Would it carry the same connotation in a third-world nation as in an industrialized one? The point is that we have developed an image of our perception of what a president looks like. If you fit that image, you may have a better chance of being elected. If you don't, well...

Saul was "the whole package." He was the son of Kish, a wealthy, influential man of the tribe of Benjamin. He is described as "the most handsome man in Israel" and stood head-and-shoulders above everyone else. Money, looks, stature – yes, he was the complete package. You couldn't miss him in a crowd. If there ever was someone as marketable for the position of King, Saul was it. However, as we will see in our review of his life as a leader, those very persuasive externals masked some glaring internal deficiencies that ultimately proved to be the seeds which produced the downfall of a leader who was presented with the opportunity of a lifetime.

Apple Tree or Christmas Tree?

One of the things we did while raising our family was to go apple picking at a local orchard during the Fall each year. We made a day of it. I can remember picking a ripe, delicious apple from a tree and biting into it, tasting how sweet it was. This was followed by fresh apple cider at the onsite store, not to mention the freshly baked apple doughnuts as well. I can still smell them.

One of my favorite times of the year is Christmas. We celebrate Christmas by decorating a tree in our home with beautiful ornaments and lights. In fact, we use certain ornaments that tell the history of the growth of our family. It warms my heart just to think about those memories.

There is a big difference between a Christmas tree and an apple tree. The fruit on an apple tree grows from what is *inherently contained within* an apple tree. Ornaments on a Christmas tree are external and placed upon it. We decorate the tree according to what is pleasing and appealing to us, according to our tastes and preferences. No matter how beautifully you dress up a Christmas tree, it will never bear anything edible. It lacks the inner quality, substance and capacity to bear fruit like an apple tree.

119

Leaders can be like Christmas trees or apple trees. Lots of money can be spent dressing up a leader. Seminars, classes, podcasts, webinars, books and articles can help "decorate" a leadership candidate to produce what people may be looking for in a leader. However, without the internal, substantive qualities and capacities inherent in a healthy and effective leader, our experience with that leader will prove to be unsatisfying and disappointing on many levels. Sadly, our culture has instilled this marketing mindset in us by using external appearances to convince us that the internal, inherent qualities are present. We just presume that everything is just as it appears, and we follow. This marketing mentality has an impact on leaders themselves as well. Leaders become convinced that, since we have all the necessary externals in place, people will like us and follow. After all, if people don't like us, how can they follow us? If they don't follow us, the competition will woo them from us. Once that happens, we will lose market share and influence. I think you get the picture.

The internal pressure and stress of considering these influences from our culture undermine our ability to see ourselves in a realistic way. Because of insecurity and lack of identity, we succumb to the false belief that, because we are not popular, we are not qualified and we feel inadequate. Many qualified, insecure leaders have fallen into this trap. Our culture has convinced them that they must reinvent themselves in order to appeal to those they seek to influence. Really?

We live in a fast moving, information-saturated world overloaded with images of success. It is true that we may have to re-examine and re-think how we package our products, present our services and describe the benefit to those who avail themselves of them; but here is the deception; we may have to reinvent our *product,* that is, what we do. ***We should never have to reinvent who we are.*** This mistaken thinking is the result of insecurity and the lack of identity that undermine our thinking. If left unchecked and unchallenged, it could prove to be the catalyst for potential and eventual failure in our role as leaders.

Seed of Destruction: Insecurity

I believe that King Saul struggled with insecurity all his life. As you consider this statement, you may not agree at first. After all, he led Israel's armies into victorious battles and became great. It is difficult to think of a King as insecure, especially when he has succeeded in some obvious ways. However, as we will see in the section that follows, the subtle driving force in how he made decisions and how he led was his insecurity. This was the hidden problem that caused him to fail to sustain success. This was the crack in his foundation that widened from the pressures of leadership, causing him to ultimately fail after being given such great opportunities to serve as Israel's first King.

Insecurity is defined as *a feeling of uneasiness deep down inside us that makes us feel inadequate, inferior or unworthy in some way.*

All of us deal with insecurity at some level from time to time. We may feel insecure about meeting new people, starting a new job, getting married or becoming a parent. However, we must remember that this is a normal, temporary level of insecurity that will dissipate as we move forward in these areas and gain more confidence. On the other hand, a prolonged sense of insecurity at a level that forms the basis of how we live our lives, make decisions and relate to others is not normal and is unhealthy. It is this high degree of insecurity and how it drives our behavior, especially in how we lead, that is so destructive to ourselves and others. While this topic is a vast and complicated one, which can fill a book alone, I will restrict my comments about insecurity only as far as they pertain to certain aspects of King Saul's leadership.

Evidence Of Insecurity In King Saul's Behavior

Being Withdrawn: (See 1 Samuel 10:22)

Tall and Handsome, he stood out from all others (See 1 Samuel 9:2). Why would Saul hide among the baggage at the ceremony where he was to be anointed king? One would expect that he would be front-and-center. We can surmise, with a fair amount of certainty, that he struggled with low self-esteem. Low self-esteem can undermine any leader in exercising the confidence that is required to lead well. His physical characteristics made him stand out in a crowd. He was used to getting people's attention. Low self-esteem and insecurity can combine to cripple a leader and prevent him from moving forward to fulfill his divine destiny and rise to meet the opportunities presented to him. There is an irony here. When we look at a leader who is used to being in the spotlight and in the public eye, the last thing we expect is to think that they battle with low self-esteem and insecurity. However, many do and work very hard to mask their secret struggle.

When left unresolved over time, these "cracks in the foundation" have a way of becoming exposed, despite all efforts to keep them from being known. Evidence of this can be seen by observing a leader's leadership style and the way they relate to subordinates and team members, as well as how they speak and make decisions.

It is important to pause for a moment and realize that Saul was God's CHOICE. God chooses people, not so much based upon their present status and condition, but upon the potential of what He will make of them as they learn to rely on and obey Him.

Nevertheless, a new or young leader with low self-esteem will often act in a way that SEEMS LIKE HUMILITY, but may not be. When we consider this young man who has the opportunity of a lifetime facing him *hiding,* we may think he is acting in a humble manner and that he doesn't want to be in the public eye. To the person himself, it may be a strategy often resorted to which I call a classic TAKE-AWAY. This is a manipulative tactic. You see, by hiding, he forced the people to seek him out. In the mind of the person, this acts as a defense mechanism to a fear of failure. If he failed, he could rationalize that he didn't volunteer. Rather, the people sought him out. It is an attempt to take the pressure off.

There is another additional pressure that insecure leaders feel very keenly: it is Peer Pressure. They said of Saul in 1 Samuel 10:24, *"...there's no one else like him..."* This is almost never the compliment you might expect of the insecure person. Why? Because, while the person may feel affirmed by it, the feeling is fleeting. The insecure person now feels the added emotional weight of the expectations of the people upon him and becomes anxious over whether he will be able to sustain and live up to them.

Now, let us look at how Saul made decisions and handled various events and try to gain some insight about this young man with the world at his fingertips. Several key events we will observe give us a clue as to how low self-esteem and insecurity often manifest in the conduct of a leader. They are:

How a leader handles rejection. (See 1 Samuel 10:27)

In this passage, we see a group of people who rejected Saul as King of Israel. We don't know how large the group was, but we do know they found him unacceptable. The Bible describes them as "base fellows," that is, "useless, nobodies" according to the original Biblical language. Why should their opinion matter to him?

Often, while an insecure leader may run from the spotlight, they deeply desire it. Remember, they crave acceptance. The Bible tells us that Saul "ignored" them. The word translated as ignored in the New Living Translation literally refers to "a cut, a deep engraving."

While Saul acted like there was no visible response to their rejection of him, there actually was a deep cut made within him. Their rejection caused a deep, inner wounding engraved on his soul.

This response was anything but ignoring them. This "internal bleeding" will have an impact – sooner or later. This is a crack in the foundation of the soul of a new or young leader. If left unhealed, it will have a negative impact on one's career, and it did for Israel's first King.

Leading out of anger. (See 1 Samuel 11:6-7)

This passage tells us that an enemy had come against Jabesh-Gilead, an Israelite town, to conquer it. The people were afraid and asked for time to seek help before surrendering. Saul came in from the field finding everyone crying. When he asked what the problem was, they told him about the King of Ammon and what his plans against them were. When he heard the facts, he became angry. It is important to note that the Scripture says, *"...the Spirit of the Lord came upon him, and he became angry..."* There is a very important distinction we need to realize here. There is anger in response to something that is righteous, justifiable and appropriate that comes from the Spirit of God. I am reminded of the time that Jesus entered the Temple courts and turned over all the money-changers' tables and those who sold doves (See Matthew 21:12). He was angry, but this was the appropriate response. On the other hand, there is anger that is not from God, but our own soulish natures. This kind is not appropriate, never justified and often irrational. We will see the negative expression of anger in Saul's leadership style later in this chapter. The key for us here about leading out of anger is that *we must always maintain objectivity about ourselves and the situation we find ourselves in to be able to discern when anger is and is not the appropriate response.*

Saul reacted emotionally to the emotion he witnessed in the people of the city. His anger, displayed in the act of cutting up the yoke of oxen he was plowing with, made the people "afraid." It was the FEAR OF THE LORD that God expressed through Saul, NOT THE FEAR OF SAUL. This is the positive impact of an appropriate and godly expression of anger. Leaders, like Saul, who are often led by their emotions, must be careful that they respond appropriately to difficult situations. They are representing the authority of God and should never act in such a way as to draw attention to themselves, rather than to God. Moreover, leaders need to understand that people will get their impressions and understanding about God in the way the leader portrays Him as His representative. This is true in ministry and in the family. God wants leaders to lead with an authority that directs and inspires people to fear and reverence the Lord, NOT THE LEADER.

The Performance Trap: set very subtly. (See 1 Samuel 11:12-13)

This is a very critical part of the story of Saul's leadership. Remember those "base fellows" that rejected his selection as leader? After defeating his enemies, the men around Saul now asked, *"Where are those guys now?"* I am sure they were thinking they should be brought before Saul for their treasonous act of rejection and face the music. A leader must be careful about counsel received from those working closely with them. At times, their counsel comes from the Spirit of God. At other times, they come from another source. That other source can be from their own natural inclinations, from the devil or a combination of both. I recall a time when Jesus began telling His disciples that He was soon to be betrayed, beaten and crucified. Peter came up to Him and corrected Him saying, *"Don't say things like this..."* Jesus rebukes him and says, *"...get behind me Satan, for you don't desire the things of God but the things of man."* (See Matthew 16:23).

Saul exercised discretion and humility here. His associates called for revenge, now that Saul had PROVEN

HIMSELF. This is a time when a leader can become most vulnerable to ungodly counsel. It is not at a time of experiencing defeat, but after experiencing a great victory. The lesson for leaders here is that if the devil cannot defeat you through failure, he may attempt to do so through success.

Saul declared, *"No one dies today..."* I wonder if this came from his heart to honor the Lord or to DRAW ATTENTION TO HIMSELF? Remember, his soul was still deeply engraved. I suspect his motivation was the latter. The evidence that there was no healing will be expressed later in his administration when he falls so low as to attempt to murder David because he perceives him as his competitor and rival.

Saul's popularity rose and fell on the success of his army (to him, at least). Some leaders' success rises and falls on the strength of their choir, teaching ministry or some component of their ministry organization. When that popularity is threatened or begins to fade, the insecure leader will resort to many things they thought they would never do or say before then. Therefore, a leader must acknowledge and understand that their popularity will rise and fall, but we must stay the course and continue the mission with godly integrity. Our culture gives celebrity status to leaders who perform, without regard to integrity and character. For a leader who craves the accolades, this can set him on a course to continue to seek approval by continuing to perform. We must be very careful not to fall into this trap.

Destructive Characteristics of Insecure Leadership

Disobedience due to fear: (Presumption). (See 1 Samuel 13:5-9)

The army began to desert Saul because of fear. The enemy army was growing larger and larger. The problems were getting bigger and bigger. Saul's soldiers started to desert. Remember, his army was what Saul relied upon to prop-up his being perceived as a strong and competent leader by the people. A very crucial flaw in the inner nature of Saul now became exposed. A crack in the foundation had now widened so much that a collapse was imminent. I identify this crack as Saul's holding his fear of man over his fear of God.

Saul seemed more concerned with what the people (his soldiers) thought rather than what God had spoken through the prophet Samuel. Samuel instructed Saul to wait for him to arrive before sacrificing an offering prior to entering into battle. After all, Saul wanted the blessing of God on his efforts. This is a good thing. However, as Saul's problems grew bigger and the pressures of leadership started to mount, Saul took matters into his own hands and performed the sacrifice.

Sure enough, as soon as Saul finished the sacrifice, Samuel arrived. It is important to note here that God may show up early, or He may show up late, but He is always on time. A secure leader would have waited for Samuel to perform the sacrifice. Saul could have said to himself, *"The Lord knows all things. He knew that Samuel would be late. I should still trust that He knows best, and Samuel will get here on God's timetable, not mine."*

A leader must be more concerned about how GOD is perceived in the eyes of others, rather than how the LEADER is perceived. What a testimony there could have been had Saul modeled faith to his army, rather than presumption. They would have seen what happens when a leader puts his total trust in the Lord. Sadly, he was more concerned for his own reputation than God's. A secure leader's reputation is ALWAYS EXPENDABLE, but God NEVER IS. Leaders are good at getting things done. However, we need to get them done in God's timing and in God's ways. We must never take matters into our own hands and take action, when God has already instructed us otherwise.

A feigned "spirituality." (See 1 Samuel 13:11-14)

Insecurity often drives leaders into very wrong decisions. Insecure leaders often try to camouflage it in *spiritually sounding terms* to appear sincerely interested in God's glory. Saul tells Samuel the story. He was waiting, but Samuel was late. (Note: the problem is never with God, so don't ever go there). Saul further declared that the battle was building up and *"...he hadn't asked for the Lord's help."* That sounds so spiritual, doesn't it? It wasn't. It was a hypocritical display and an act of self-deceived self-will. Samuel reprimanded him and declared that his decision was foolish. God would have established Saul's kingdom forever. Instead, the kingdom would be taken from him.

I wonder how many careers and ministry tracks have been ended because leaders took matters into their own hands after God had already spoken, suffering the loss of ministry rather than its advancement? When leaders take actions, which they are responsible to take, based upon their knowledge and experience, we call it leadership. If our limited knowledge causes a negative outcome, God may still bless our ignorance. However, when God has already given instructions on how to proceed and we do what we want to do instead, that is called rebellion. God can bless ignorance, but He will never bless rebellion.

Foolish oaths, rules and regulations – Setting up a paradigm for CONTROL.

Saul became so self-driven and fear-driven that he issued an oath to his exhausted troops. When self-willed, controlling leaders fail to gain the control they seek, they will often set ministry requirements or standards that will be hard for team members to comply with. Such standards often wear them out, exasperate and exhaust them. They demand things like, *"I want you at every service"; "You need to show up half-hour earlier for a pre-meeting meeting"; "I need you to take on additional responsibilities. I know it's a challenge, but this is ministry."* The list goes on and on.

Saul made a foolish oath (See 1 Samuel 14). His troops were exhausted because he was driving them constantly. They needed rest and hadn't eaten, yet, Saul issued a decree that a *"...curse would fall on anyone who ate any food before Saul had a chance to get revenge on his enemy."* This is a classic example of destructive control. He had his agenda and wanted those who battled alongside him to not rest until what HE wanted was accomplished. This is controlling and manipulative behavior. His soldiers needed rest and food, but he kept pressuring them to get it done.

A secure leader allows, even insists, that his soldiers get the rest they need and eat like they should. How does this apply to our leadership style today? Well, are you making sure your leaders are practicing Sabbath? Are you giving them the chance to rest and refresh themselves? Are you ensuring that they are "eating?" Are they benefitting from being nourished in the Word, so they can continue serving with strength? When this is not the case, many staff members and fellow leaders are left hungry and frustrated, which will result in spiritual decline and ineffectiveness. As leaders, we must ask ourselves, *"Are my fellow workers and leaders getting fed as much as the people they are feeding?"*

The non-negotiable principle that is violated when this happens is this: **People are more important than programs.**

Failure to live by this principle will frustrate staff, create breakdowns in them and their family relationships and result in increased turnover among staff. Ministries will start and stop constantly under a leadership that fails to maintain this principle. Furthermore, this will result in bringing division among the staff, for example, Jonathan and his men versus Saul. It will undermine the leader's authority, because he will be faced with having to reverse a decision he made. This happened when Saul discovered that Jonathan had eaten something. Now, should his own son be cursed? All the people around Saul pleaded with him to spare his son who had won a victory that day. It was embarrassing, but that was Saul's fault. (See 1 Samuel 14:44-46).

A healthy leader must always check his leadership practice and ask, *"Am I leading in accordance with the principles I and this ministry stand for?"* For example, if we say, *"We're all about family,"* but don't allow our team to spend more time with theirs, something is wrong. If we say, *"We're all about spending more quality time with the Lord in prayer and study,"* but call staff to an inordinately large number of meetings all week, something is wrong. If we say, *"We're all about the quality of life and ministry and not quantity,"* but continue to jam the church calendar with programs and activities, something is wrong.

You may be thinking, *"But there are so many needs of the people to be tended to. How will all of that get done?"* I believe the answer is simpler than you may think at first. Jesus said, *"The poor you will always have with you, but you won't always have me with you."* (See Matthew 26:11, Mark 14:7 & John 12:8). I believe Jesus was saying, *"There will always be needs."* There will always be counseling, training, sick calls, births and other needs. When He said, *"But ME you will not always have"* I believe He was speaking about relationships and priorities that may someday pass and you will never be able to recapture them. A leader must think about this for himself, his family and the leaders and their families serving with him. Leader, you will never get a second chance to go to your child's first birthday party. You will never get another chance to go to their graduation from kindergarten. You will never get a second chance to see their first soccer game, and neither will your team for their families. We have all heard that sometimes "less is more." In ministry, less is almost always more. Let us strive to build deeper, rather than wider. Let us esteem people higher than programs. Let us release people and ourselves from the bondage of misplaced control.

Leading by the demands of the people is not always the same as being Spirit-Led. The insecure leader's judgment is clouded where he assumes that his decisions are God's by default. ***Just because you CAN do something, doesn't mean you should. Just because God doesn't stop you or immediately discipline you, doesn't mean He approves of your decisions.***

The Impact Of Insecurity On Leadership Development

I have already mentioned that I suspected Saul struggled with low self-esteem. Evidence of this is clearly described in his conversation with Samuel (See 1 Samuel 9:21). He described himself as the least person in the smallest family in the smallest tribe in Israel. Naturally, his question to Samuel was, *"Why are you speaking like this to me?"* Low self-esteem plays a key role as a trigger for Saul's disobedience and rationalization toward selfishness and personal gain under the cloak of religious zeal. His self-promoting and self-rewarding tendency is a problem that many other leaders experience in their struggle with low self-esteem.

We often fail to recognize this, however, mainly because we associate monetary gain or ministry advancement with strong leadership, spiritual power and approval by God. This is NOT always the case. We see many celebrity ministers today who manage enormous budgets and large ministries as secure and having it all together. However, they may still struggle with insecurity and low self-esteem. The people's choice of a king was dependent upon the outer appearance, the externals, and the optics. How many of us have heard the question, *"So, how large is your church?"* when meeting another leader for the first time? Let's remember that God looks upon the HEART when He chooses a leader, not on the size of his ministry.

An insecure leader needs to be perceived by the people as the one who is the best minister. He or she must be the best speaker, teacher or counselor. If they cannot, then they will try to take the credit for others on their team who excel in an area more than they do. Leadership development under this kind of leader will be practically non-existent. I believe this is what was behind Saul asking David to wear his armor when going out to fight against Goliath (See 1 Samuel 17). Had David worn Saul's armor going out to confront Goliath, everyone would have been watching from afar and thought that it was Saul confronting the giant. An insecure leader will often speak of upcoming leaders as the ones "they discovered" or "mentored," somehow attempting to make it appear that their growth would not have happened without them.

Insecurity was so deeply ingrained in Saul's soul that, even after he is told that the Lord had rejected him as king, he asks Samuel to accompany him back to worship *"to honor me before the elders of Israel and the people"* (See 1 Samuel 15:30-31). God's criteria for leadership is found in 1 Samuel 16:7. The Lord doesn't consider the externals or the optics when He chooses a leader; He looks on the heart.

When a leader who battles insecurity doesn't address it and work on getting help, other issues can develop. Like weeds in a beautiful garden, these items can multiply quickly, having greater negative impact on the leader and the organization.

Doors Are Opened to Demonic Influence

It is interesting to note that the *"...Spirit of the Lord had left Saul and a tormenting spirit now vexed him..."* (See 1 Samuel 16:14). When a void is created in the heart of a leader, it can open the door to the enemy. This is probably the most glaring example of how wrong things could go when a leader persists in being driven by low self-esteem and insecurity. The enemy of our souls (satan) takes advantage of these openings to bring confusion and strife into the leader and the organization. Jesus said that the enemy comes to steal, kill and destroy (See John 10:10). This could have been avoided if Saul had been humble, broken and contrite and in an accountable relationship with someone, for example, Samuel. When the "torment" is in the leader, the rest of the "body" is at risk of demonic influences that enter in through this open door.

Leadership has consequences, negative and positive, demonic and godly. This is one reason why untried, immature people should not be given leadership roles solely dependent upon their gifting. We must be sure leadership candidates are whole within. This way, they will be able to sustain the pressures of ministry successfully. Gifting will only carry you so far. Cracks in the foundation of our souls will widen under pressure of leadership and can result in the collapse in the leader, the team and possibly the organization.

Using people and valuing things. (See 1 Samuel 16:22-23)

When leaders get caught up in the momentum and daily pace of ministry demands, it becomes easy to forget their priorities. The demands of ministry are relative. That is, they may differ in scope depending on the skill set of the leader, his gifting and the size of the ministry. However, any leader in each situation is susceptible to becoming so consumed with the business of ministry that they can lose sight of what really matters. A leader can easily fall into the snare of focusing on function rather than on people. Saul is a typical example. A tormenting spirit was vexing Saul at this time in his life, so his leaders advised him to have someone come play music for him in an effort to calm him. Somehow, they knew that David played the harp skillfully and called for him. David's father sent him to Saul to serve him with his gift. David succeeded in his mission and became Saul's armor bearer. In fact, Saul loved David. Saul welcomed David's "gift," but ONLY to the extent that it MET HIS OWN PERSONAL NEED. It wouldn't be long before Saul would perceive David as his competitor and enemy. An entire series of events would soon lead up to that. I would like to make a special note here. Jesus, in His sermon on the mount, describe the principles of how the Kingdom of God operates. It starts small, like a mustard seed, but grows to have majority influence becoming the greatest tree in the garden. This same principle applies to the development of a ministry and a leader. Our gifts and ministry may start with small beginnings but will grow over time to have major influence. This works both positively and negatively. This principle of progressive development is seen in the life of Saul. He started out well, but he didn't finish well. The negative issues he faced as an individual (a seed) would ultimately affect the entire nation in a negative way.

Insecure leaders welcome gifted team members, but they are often primarily concerned with how that gift makes them or their ministries appear to the public or the rest of the team. David's ministry gift benefitted Saul. It added value to his court.

When leaders get swept up in the throes of ministry, they can easily fall into the trap of valuing a person's function, rather than the person themselves. There are always ministry meetings to attend. There are numerous strategy sessions, surveys, SWOT analyses, etc. SWOT Analysis is a useful technique for understanding your strengths and weaknesses, and for identifying both the opportunities open to you and the threats you face.[1] While these may be valuable tools to improve ministry, leaders must be sure they are spending more time improving people. When leaders focus on equipping leaders to grow personally and fulfill their destiny in God's plan for them, the leader's ministry will grow in response. Remember, people are more important than things. Love people and use things. Never use people and love things.

The spirit of CONTROL and the need to BRAND all ministries. (See 1 Samuel 17)

We are all familiar with this great, defining event in the life of David and the history of Israel. However, there are very telling and subtle aspects in this story that are symptoms of control, creating an adversarial atmosphere in Saul's court. As David prepared to go out to confront the giant, Saul suggested he wear Saul's own armor. This may seem like an effort by Saul to protect David. However, I am convinced that this was because the people who saw this from a distance would think it was Saul who defeated Goliath.

---

[1] https://www.mindtools.com/pages/article/newTMC_05.htm

We are living in a culture that markets everything. As a result, branding has become the mantra of our generation. Therefore, to sustain success, the brand must be on everything. Whether it is a slogan or the picture of the founder, EVERYTHING must be branded. We don't speak of ministry organizations in terms of anointing any longer. After all, it is the anointing on the leader that "breaks the yoke." The anointing is the key element of a ministry resulting in spiritual power. Spiritual power is transformational; it changes people. A marketed brand never changed anyone's life. Today, ministries are known more by their branding and resulting popularity. Marketing has taken the lead in ministry development. The experience of participating in the execution of well-marketed ministry is the all-important focus. As a result, we draw more "consumers" and grab more "market share," causing our ministry to grow. However, not all growth is God's growth. I am persuaded that the prevalence of this characteristic is a low point in the ministry of the church today.

The book of Acts describes the practice of the Apostles centered on the person of Jesus Christ and the demonstrable power of the Holy Spirit. It was the key quality of the early church and the ministry of Paul and the other Apostles. After all, it was Paul who told the church in Corinth that, *"...his ministry was not in the words that man's wisdom teaches, but in the demonstration of the Spirit and power, so that your faith would be in the power of God rather than the wisdom of man."* (See 1 Corinthians 2:4-5). Perhaps we should re-examine our methodologies and return to their example.

An insecure leader is easy prey to a marketing mindset. The drive to grow the ministry, bring in funds and increase the reach of ministry drives decisions that may be at odds with the Biblical pattern. An anointed, but insecure leader will want his name or image to be on all that a ministry does. Success is what we all desire in ministry. However, letting the desire for it drive ministry may prove to be a snare for us and cause us to forfeit anointing. When an insecure leader makes the mistake of thinking it is him who brings success, he becomes the "brand" of the ministry. I doubt that this meets with the Lord's approval, and it prohibits the growth and development of any other leader beyond a certain point in the organization.

Insecure Leaders will often seek AFFIRMATION by AFFILIATION. (See 1 Samuel 18:2)

David was successful in defeating Goliath. Saul now kept David with him and would not allow him to return home. It is important to celebrate victory with team members and associates in ministry. However, a leader must be careful to give honor and celebrate the person himself, without insinuating that it was "because of me" that the team member succeeded. Secure leaders give away praise in large doses. They don't mind a team member becoming popular because of his anointing.

An insecure leader, fearing failure, will often surround themselves with strong, successful leaders in an attempt to gain affirmation by association with them.

Often, there will be name-dropping, photos taken (and prominently displayed for all to see), and "friendships" made with other leaders. While all this is not a problem in itself, the problem can arise when the reason for all of it is to cover or overcome some deep wound, insecurity or fear. I believe that this hidden agenda in Saul was the seed that resulted in his jealousy of David. As David's successes mounted and his popularity increased, the people sang his praises. *"Saul has killed his thousands, but David his ten thousands"* was their song. This became a serious problem for Saul.

Let the (Jealousy) games begin. (See 1 Samuel 18)

In a secure leader, success of others is celebrated. For an insecure leader, success that leads to increased popularity by a co-laborer will be viewed with jealousy. Every secure "father" wants his son or daughter to out-succeed him. No parent would resent the success of a son or daughter unless there were serious underlying issues that remain unhealed or unresolved in that parent.

If the insecurity is not healed and the leader does not overcome it, it will overcome the leader at the expense of other team members and the ministry. An insecure leader will measure the successes of team members with a view towards how it makes the leader look. In this kind of atmosphere, suspicion, control, lying, deception and murmuring fester. Other leaders on the team may clearly perceive the "600-pound gorilla in the room," but never say a word about it or address it in an effort to resolve it. This creates an unsafe environment for growth, anointing or the blessing of God. If this condition is allowed to persist over a long period of time, a cycle of constant turnover will ensue. Good people will continually enter and leave the organization, always taking pieces of it with them.

Paradox: Increased success engenders more and more fear in an insecure leader (See 1 Samuel 18:14-15).

One would think this would help the leader recognize God's hand on the successful team member. However, insecurity often blinds the leader from seeing God's hand.

In fact, it won't be long until the successful team member is cast into a negative light. Insecure leaders will resort to distorting the facts and manipulation to exert control over others in the organization who sympathize with the "Davids."

Game: Establish relationship to exert CONTROL.
(See 1 Samuel 18:17)

Marrying into the family will give Saul influence over David, so he could control him more. Saul used his daughter as leverage. Often, an insecure leader will place an upcoming leader on their team, only so they could exert some level of control over them. An anointed team member, gaining favor with the people because they have favor with God, may breed jealousy in an insecure leader. That leader may seek to hire the person and put them on staff. There is nothing necessarily wrong with that. However, you cannot fire a person unless you hire them first. To eliminate the perceived competition, insecure leaders will hold the new staff member to various rules and regulations, hoping they will fail. In this way, they will be rid of the competition, but under the guise of innocence in the process. (See 1 Samuel 18:20-25)

Game: Using loyal people to ensnare innocent ones.

Saul sends his servants to tell David, *"The king really likes you."* (1 Samuel 18:22). Saul is trying to ensnare David and is prepared to SET HIM UP FOR FAILURE!

Unfortunately, loyal staff members are often unsuspectingly taken-in by an insecure leader. Many times, the spirit of control operating in that organization will make those team members "feel disloyal," if they don't report back everything they see and hear. This loss of objectivity causes division to spread like a cancer in the organization and threatens to eventually destroy it.

Game: Setting people up for failure. (1 Samuel 18:25)

Saul asks for 100 Philistine foreskins as a dowry, but his purpose was to see David killed in battle. Insecure leaders will often place unbearable pressure and burdensome requirements on staff to foster failure. They could then dismiss them for it, but the motive is jealousy. Work hours, attendance at numerous meetings, attendance at multiple services and other pressures are piled up on gifted staff who are regarded with jealousy. In this way, when the staff member leaves, they are cited as having failed to divert blame from the leader.

Often, the very manipulative statement, *"This is ministry"* is used as an excuse. This is neither modeled nor taught anywhere in the Bible.

Doing the devil's work for him. (See 1 Samuel 19:1)

The effects of Saul's behavior up to this time have brought him and his court (organization) to a very sad state. Jesus said that the *"...thief comes to steal, KILL and destroy..."* (See John 10:10). Here we see Saul ordering the assassination of David. The foothold that was presented to the enemy by an unhealed insecurity has now grown into full-fledged demonic strategy, hatched in the place where it should have been battled. Saul's attitude toward David went from loving him to wanting him killed. What a tragic development in the life of a leader who began with so much promise and potential.

A spirit of confusion – flip/flopping in extremes – DOUBLE MINDEDNESS and FALSE SECURITY.

Jonathan reminds Saul of all the good David had done. Saul stops pursuing David, and he comes back into the court (See 1 Samuel 19:4-7). The spears just keep on flying; Saul is still demonized.

When the insecure leader fails to get the help he needs, he will just vacillate between alternating positions. This gives a false sense of security to staff and the targeted team member. HERE IS WHERE DISCERNMENT IS NEEDED. It is a tactic of the enemy to feign peace and reconciliation while the (insecure) leader has not shown (demonstrably) that he has received healing. There must be "fruit for repentance" before trust can be re-established.

The remedy here is for boundaries to be established on both sides. It is not a "sin" to establish parameters through which responsibilities can be carried out.

Look out for "spears." They may come in the form of emails, but their intention is to eliminate "David." You don't need to wait for a series of spears to be hurled at you. Have the sense to realize that one is enough and RUN. There is no negotiating with a spear-thrower working for the devil. If you are the one at whom the "spear" was thrown, don't ask for "confirmations." Get out. This is where an accountable relationship with someone else will be of great benefit to you. You should have been discussing and praying together about the situation. This will provide you with a "witness" regarding the process you are engaged in. This is a very difficult thing to experience, but the Lord and your witness know the truth.

A Word to the "Davids" on the run.

Never seek the harm of the insecure leader. Don't return evil for evil. This causes you to become susceptible to the same snare the leader has fallen into. Never backbite or slander the leader. If you can't bless, don't say anything. If you do speak, speak of the leader's strengths and accomplishments. Broadcasting an insecure leader's failings will have a very negative impact on everything. It opens you up to condemnation and guilt from the enemy. It also prevents the insecure leader from repenting, and others will always see him as "that leader." This is obstructionist to the restoration/reconciliation process. Don't do the enemy's work for him by falling into this snare. Trust God to keep His word to you. Every prophecy you received will come to pass. God knew the spears would fly when He gave you those words. He who *"watches over His Word to perform it"* (See Jeremiah 1:12) will do so for you. It is not a matter of **FACT**: it's just a matter of **TIME**.

Seven Strategies For Dealing With Insecurity

1. **Understand what you are feeling and why.**

   a. What could be the root causes of these feelings?

   b. Are they VALID causes that result in insecurity?

   c. There is hope to overcome it.

   d. Seek the help of a professional counselor. You will receive the necessary "tools" to help you. "Self-medicating" is a bad idea.

2. **Take Steps to GROW.**

   a. Prayerfully consider partnering with someone to form an accountable relationship. This is someone who loves you and will tell you the truth, even if you don't like it. They possess the objectivity you are lacking.

   b. Take small steps and believe for them to become larger as you move forward. Don't despise the day of small beginnings. Remember, the kingdom progresses like the mustard seed in Matthew 13.

3. Remove your "security blanket."

    a. Start doing things differently. Insecure leaders often use "busyness" to hide their fears of personal contact with others. Call someone, rather than email. Meet them, rather than call them. Change may be uncomfortable, but it will help you and is necessary to break out of the trap of insecurity. Become reachable again. When a ministry is too big for a senior leader to relate to a team member personally, the ministry is too big. You cannot delegate relationship.

    b. Don't rely on titles or function. Be real and transparent – or at least try to be. Practice will get you there. After all, you have been practicing insecurity up to now. Trust the Lord to sustain you in this process.

4. Change your perspective.

    a. Stop listening to the wrong people.
    b. Stop watching the news, if it feeds your insecurity.
    c. Move on to more positive influences in your environment.

    d. Practice Philippians 4:8-9.

5. Do what you know best to do.

    a. Increase practicing what you are good at.

    b. Celebrate your competencies and the gifts and abilities of OTHERS.

    c. "The most anointed you is YOU." Stop trying to be someone else.

6. Reward Improvements.

    a. Love yourself first, then others. On an airline, the safety announcement informs us that we are to put our oxygen mask on first, the we will be able to help others. Take care of YOU.

    b. Set goals: realistic, measurable and achievable. Share them with your team to keep you accountable.

    c. Reward yourself for achieving them.

    d. Keep your accountability partner(s) in the loop.

7. **Keep a journal.**

    a. Enter your thoughts, words, prayers, goals, etc.

    b. Read your entries periodically – how do you sound? Do you sound better now than you did when you began? That is called progress.

    c. A journal will enable you to see and measure your progress.

Conclusion

The treatment of King Saul's insecurity and the destruction it caused him, and the kingdom, can only be partially addressed here. However, there are three main lessons we can learn from him to help us avoid his fate:

1. **Obey God and seek to do His will.**

    a. Seek Him with a whole heart (He must be FIRST PRIORITY).

    b. Obey what He directs you to do (written or prophetic words).

    c. Align with His will for YOUR life, not anyone else's. (See Matthew 10:32).

2. Don't abuse/misuse the authority given to you.

    a. Our authority is DELEGATED, it is not inherently ours. Steward it with care.

    b. If failure doesn't defeat us, success may. Pride is a slow killer. Avoid "celebrity status" and "star treatment." How? REFUSE IT.

    c. Remind yourself of Luke 17:10 – we are ALL unprofitable servants; doing only what is our DUTY to do.

3. Pursue a godly leadership model.

    a. While the ministry has a "business" side to it, that doesn't mean that leaders need to be CEOs. We need to be "spiritual mothers and fathers" to a generation and "parent" them into the Kingdom of God.

    b. Find a spiritual father who can parent you as you develop in leadership. Find a mentor who will challenge you to grow.

    c. Follow 1 Peter 5:2-10:

Eleven steps to successful leadership:

1. Care for the flock first, not yourself.

2. Watch over it protectively with a pure heart.
3. Don't lord your authority over your team. Be the leader you want to follow.
4. There is a crown awaiting the "bowed head" of fruitful wheat.
5. Practice servant leadership. This is the Jesus way.
6. Humble yourself (or God will, out of love for you).
7. Give Him all your anxieties (don't let them DRIVE you).
8. Stay alert! Discernment is the key.
9. Stand firm. Once you have done all you know to do, don't act until God directs again. Waiting is hard, but worth it. Don't take things into your own hands when God "delays."
10. Be strong in the faith. Word, worship and serving others are key as you build yourself up in the Lord.
11. Become "other-oriented." It is not about YOU: it's about being Christ like. He sought the welfare of others first and reaped in abundance in return.

No leader who ends up like Saul ever started off that way. Saul's story is that of a person who was presented with the opportunity of a lifetime. However, he never fulfilled his destiny in the plan of God. His struggle with insecurity was a main issue that, because it was never resolved, grew to become a destructive agent that affected his entire life.

Saul was a leader who did not know his identity. His low self-esteem, over time, caused him to seek identity in the things he did. He found affirmation in the approval of others. This became a motivating force in his life. The principle of progressive development, as cited earlier in this chapter, works in a negative or positive way. We see in Saul's life how it worked negatively. Insecurity, or any issue we struggle with, must be dealt with as soon as we become aware of it. The "snowball effect" that an unhealed "crack" in our inner foundation can have on our lives is greater than we may think. Every individual's life may not have the impact that Saul's had. The thing to realize is that an unhealed wound in our souls WILL have an impact on our entire world. It extended to a nation, because Saul occupied a national position and function. Our "world" may be drastically smaller, but the negative impact will be made on all of it eventually.

Our identity must be found primarily in our relationship with God through Christ. We must learn to derive strength, confidence and affirmation from our Heavenly Father, as Christ did. When we do, it won't matter what our jobs, positions or statuses are. We will be able to endure change. We will become flexible and adjust to any situation. We will be emotionally healthy leaders leading emotionally healthy teams.

A Word About Spiritual Fathers

Even though I have been describing the problems and challenges that leaders struggle with, I want to caution the reader not to be so quick to make application to those you are serving with in leadership over you. Despite their shortcomings, spiritual sons and daughters are obliged to honor their spiritual fathers and mothers. Regardless of their deficiencies, the fact remains that God has placed us under the authority of imperfect spiritual parents. As such, in covenant with them and the Lord who appointed them, we owe them our deepest respect. We should speak of them with honor. We should be like David. When he heard that Saul fell on his sword in battle, he said, *"Don't tell the story in Gath."* This was a city of the Philistines; Israel's enemy. David wanted to protect the reputation of his king, even to the end of his life. When we dishonor the leadership God has placed over us, we make an announcement to the enemies of the Gospel which they will gloat over. Let us always strive to deprive them of that opportunity.

159

Profile 6: King David

Becoming A Leader After God's Own Heart.

Key Scripture: Acts 13:22

Leaders are not perfect. Leaders are not born: they are made. David's life and his ascendency to become the King of Israel stands in stark contrast to the life of his predecessor, King Saul. David was a warrior, a shepherd, a musician and writer. He was creative and sensitive to the things of God. David was a great leader. He was considered a man "after God's own heart." (See 1 Samuel 13:14).

While entire books have been written about the life of David, I will focus on his role as a leader and how he handled certain crucial situations in his life. Saul was a leader who derived his sense of value from his accomplishments and strove to find his identity in them. David, on the other hand, found his value, sense of esteem and identity from his relationship to the Lord, his God. For me, David was a leader whose focus was on being and becoming, rather than doing and accomplishing. This is not to say that accomplishments are not important. I simply mean that they cannot be the only things that define who we are. Accomplishments are temporary, but identity found in relationship to an eternal God transcends the ups and downs of this life and are eternal. It was David's internal qualities, rather than his accomplishments, that made him a man after God's own heart.

An illustration I often use to describe the importance of our inner life is what I call *The Toothpaste Test*. What happens when you squeeze a tube of toothpaste? Toothpaste comes out, of course. Why? *Because that's what is inside.* When the circumstances and challenges of life "squeeze" a leader, it will become quickly evident what is inside. Integrity, morality, faithfulness, loyalty and other qualities will become evident, despite external pressures or other people's opinions. On the other hand, jealousy, envy, bitterness, anger, pride, self-will and arrogance may come out.

I find it very interesting that, when considering all the things that happened in David's life - the mistakes he made, sins he committed, his flawed parenting and his self-reliance – he is still known in Scripture as a "man after God's own heart." Is this the work of a Jewish scribe who wanted to leave the reputation of Israel's most famous king untainted? No, this is how the Holy Spirit has chosen to remember him. This is intentional and not a scribal preference. In this profile, I will attempt to list certain qualities of the life of David that I believe contributed to him being remembered as he is. While each of these items listed could fill a book themselves, I will only cover them briefly. Perhaps you will be able to glean an understanding of what makes a leader a man after

God's own heart and put the same qualities into practice in your own lives.

A Resume With Only One Entry

Priorities are important. They can tell us a lot about a person. Observing a person's life – how he spends his time, talent and treasure – provides clues to what that person considers a priority in his life.

How are priorities developed? Well, certainly they are shaped by the urgencies of the matters at hand for a leader. There is always something to do. There is always someone who needs help. There is always an "emergency," perceived or real. There are numerous and varied issues that come up in our day-to-day lives as leaders that pull on us. We do our best to assemble them in order of urgency – usually "on the run"- and deal with them as best we could. When we succumb to this paradigm of leading an organization, ministry or family, we will soon find ourselves on the road to burnout.

Our resume is a chronology of all our accomplishments. It tells people what qualifies us for the position we aim to occupy in applying for a job. David had a resume with one entry. That is, he had one, overarching priority that marked his life and his leadership. His first priority was his desire for the Lord and his passion to know Him more and more intimately. In Psalm 27:4, David wrote, *"One thing have I desired of the Lord; that I will seek after; to behold the beauty of the Lord and enquire in His temple."* This priority is comparable to the command of Jesus in Matthew 6:33, where He said, *"But seek first the Kingdom of God and His righteousness..."*

I realize that you may be thinking this is a little unrealistic. *"Of course, this is what all leaders desire,"* you may be thinking. You may think that having to deal with the hectic pace of your schedule, this is almost impossible to practice regularly. We rationalize, *"Surely, I do this whenever I get the chance or when time and energy permit."* The problem is, time and energy and our schedules very rarely permit this. You see, when we maintain this attitude toward our relationship with the Lord, we play a game of deception with ourselves. Let us take the priority of prayer for example. Anyone asked would agree wholeheartedly that prayer is a major priority. However, if I asked you to list how you spent the last twenty-four hours, placing an activity alongside the time spent on it, how much time would prayer occupy? I believe you get the point. Our good intentions, without appropriate, deliberate actions, only keep the game going. In the life of a leader, this could have very dangerous consequences to him and those he is leading.

What are your priorities? More specifically, what are your *non-negotiables*? That is, what are those priorities that you will maintain, regardless of the pressures facing you daily in your role as a leader? These are specific priorities that you will practice, to which all others will be subject. Having non-negotiable priorities means that you will change everything else to conform to practicing them first and practicing them best. Everything else will be at the expense of these non-negotiables. Is the first one your relationship and desire for the Lord?

The significance of this cannot be overstated. When God rejected Saul as Israel's king and told Samuel that he found a man after his own heart to take his place, he was speaking about David. This is remarkable to me. God rejected a man who had some very significant accomplishments and victories under his belt. Instead, he chose someone with a less impressive resume (in man's eyes) whom He knew would serve Him in a way that glorified Him best. This is one of the greatest treasures of leadership to have. It was this priority and desire that kept the inner life of David intact, even though things he did (his outer life) were sometimes so destructive and harmful.

The following is my list of leadership qualities and practices of David that gave evidence of him being a "man after God's own heart."

Become a Lifetime Learner

Leaders like David learn to draw something out of every experience they have and recognize it as a "teaching opportunity" from God. When walking in daily relationship with the Lord, realizing, as David did, that all our days are written in His book, we learn not to complain. Instead, we learn to ask, *"Lord, what are you trying to teach me through this experience?"* This is a great act of faith and trust in the Lord. When we know that He has ordered our steps and that He goes before His sheep to lead and guide them, we will never perceive any experience as accidental. That is not to say that we have no choice in the matter. We should learn to make good, godly choices consistently. However, when the unexpected happens, we turn to God and ask, *"How can I turn this into something that will strengthen me and make me a better leader?"* David believed that those who put their trust in the Lord would never be put to shame (See Psalm 25:3). He believed that EVERY CIRCUMSTANCE he faced would ultimately work to glorify God and benefit him in some way.

Make Loneliness Your Mentor

We have all heard it said that, *"It's lonely at the top."* This means that leadership, in many ways, is a lonely place to be at times. There are times when we must take a stand and make decisions that may not be popular, but we know they are what God has said. Leaders lead. Sometimes we do so with no one standing out front with us. Loneliness, however, can be turned into our mentor. What do I mean by this?

A leader's heart is forged in the fires of adversity. Adverse circumstances, situations and numerous challenges face leaders all the time. The pressure they exert on a leader has a formative influence on a leader's heart. However, I believe that loneliness is the most difficult, but most valued mentor in our lives. Loneliness will make demands of us that other things will not. Problems may drain our energy, test our resolve or consume our intellect. A leader usually faces these things together with his ministry team or co-leaders. Loneliness, by definition, is something we cannot share with others, even a spouse. It forces us to the most difficult confrontation of our lives. It forces us to confront ourselves. Loneliness forces introspection that busy schedules and activities will deprive us of.

Damian Smeragliuolo

Loneliness Shapes Our Hearts

There were many opportunities that David had when he
was alone with God tending his father's sheep. He had
time to think, to evaluate, to dig within his own heart and
examine who he was and what he believed. In addition,
there were experiences he had that no one saw but he and
God. These shaped and prepared him for one of the
biggest moments in his life. I am referring to his battles
with the lion and the bear. He told Saul, when first hearing
Goliath's rants against Israel and her God, *"Your servant
rescued a sheep from the paw of the lion and the bear.
This uncircumcised Philistine will be like them."* (My
paraphrase. See 1 Samuel 17). You see, it was what David
battled in times alone that prepared him for battles that he
would fight in the public eye. God uses the battles that
only He and we are aware of. These must be waged, and
they must be won. When they are, God uses them to put
us in the spotlight to glorify Him on a larger scale. A
leader may complain, waiting for his "big break," for his
"golden opportunity" to put him and his ministry on the
map. The big breaks and golden opportunities come in
times of loneliness; in battles that only God and we are
aware of. These are the true golden opportunities that we
cannot afford to squander.

I believe that there were three battles David had out of the sight of the public. There was the lion, the bear and himself. I wonder which was the most difficult foe? What are the "lions" and "bears" in your own life? What are the private predators that you face? They may be wounds from your past, hurts inflicted by those you committed to serving or betrayals you have experienced by those you walked closely with and trusted fully. Sometimes these can also be fears we secretly battle that generate feelings of oppression and dread in our lives. We may be able to maintain a "victorious" façade, but inwardly cry out for deliverance from them.

It may be beneficial to mention the difference between lions and bears as predators. They both are very fierce and dangerous predators. They both evoke fear. However, they attack in different ways. Lions are stealthy hunters. They lie in wait and pounce upon their victims when they are most unaware of their presence. The "lions" a leader battles may be inner hurts or wounds that may have stemmed from childhood experiences. We may not even be aware that they exist. However, situations in our lives suddenly create an opening for them to spring upon us to devour us. The "bears" in our lives are different. Bears are lumbering attackers. No stealth tactics here. They just keep on coming until they come upon their prey, clawing and crushing them. The "bears" in a leader's life are the traumatic experiences that suddenly come upon us. There is no warning. There is no gradual experience, but a sudden, shocking onset. Traumatic experiences overwhelm us. Like a bear attack, no sooner may we hear the bear, but that he is barreling towards us, and it seems like nothing can stop him.

Like David, we must battle our lions and bears in private. We do so depending totally on the Lord and His ability to enable us to endure the process. This may require some counseling, mentoring or coaching by a trusted third party. Rest assured, God wants us to get the victory over our lions and bears. He knows there are public battles awaiting us for which He plans to give us the victory. The lions and bears are the "inner cracks" in our foundations that need to be healed. They are areas in our souls that need to be restored. Once that is accomplished, we will be enabled to withstand the pressures of facing our giants. When we do, we will be victorious.

Be Faithful In What is Another's

This is a principle of ministry that many people often miss or gloss over. Jesus tells us that *"If we are faithful in a little, God will give us much...If we are faithful in what is another's, God will give us our own."* (See Luke

16:10,12). David was tending his father's sheep when Samuel went to Jesse's home to anoint the next king of Israel. In fact, when David went to the battlefield where he heard Goliath's railings against Israel for the first time, he was tending his father's sheep. The Bible tells us that he *"left his sheep in the hand of another shepherd"* before leaving for the battlefield to bring provisions to his brothers. David was faithful in what was another's. Eventually, God gave him his own, and it was the nation.

We live in a culture of "instant everything." We want it quickly. We want to access it quickly. Yes, our access to information may be able to influence our intelligence, but an emotionally healthy leader must also have his heart and character influenced, if he is to be successful. The inward characteristics of leadership are forged by experience. They are shaped in the often-difficult process of being faithful in what is another's, before receiving your own. This is where integrity and honor are cultivated. This is how maturity in leadership is produced. During this process of being in the fire, the dross of a leader's heart is melted away. This leaves a purified heart in the leader, which will be the single, most important qualifier of his ability to lead. When speaking to leaders and leadership candidates, I always state that, *"You can teach technical and mechanical information to people, but you cannot teach character."* I would rather have a poorly taught leadership candidate with character, rather than a well-taught one without it.

Don't Judge By The Outer Appearance Of Things

I find it so interesting how David was missing from the family when Samuel went to Jesse's house to anoint Israel's next king. All of David's brothers were informed of the meeting and they prepared themselves for it. I am sure they wore their best garments and geared themselves up with their best attitudes in preparing to meet the prophet. When Samuel arrived, David was missing. Once Samuel went through the process of viewing all the sons of Jesse, he asked, *"Is there anyone else?"* Jesse said that his youngest son was in the field with the sheep. Can you imagine what David must have felt like when he found out that he wasn't even invited to that meeting?

When Samuel began to view Jesse's sons, he said, *"Surely, this is the one"* for each of them. God kept saying, *"No, not this one."* God then followed with a statement that, I believe, became a formative principle in David's life and service. God cautioned Samuel not to look on the outer appearance. He was told that God doesn't choose a leader on that basis. Instead, God looks on the heart. Once David came in, Samuel anointed him as God's choice to be Israel's next king.

As David's life progressed and developed, we can observe things on an external basis that didn't look like David was doing very well. He gathered a group of ex-cons, debtors and runaway slaves around him and lived in a cave at Adullum. That doesn't look like success, but it was. That group would give rise to the leaders who would later be known as "David's Mighty Men." A person anointed to be Israel's king would never live in a cave. Samuel must have made a mistake. No, there was no mistake. David would eventually transfer from the cave to the palace. When David informed King Saul that he would kill Goliath, Saul said, *"You're just a youth, and he's a warrior from his youth."* But David killed Goliath using what he knew and what he believed about his God.

We must also learn not to make our decisions based on outward appearances. Instead, we must prayerfully discern a leader's heart. In this day of marketing overload and survey dependence, we have become enamored with the optics of any situation. We fall for the "look" of something, rather than the substance. This practice can be tragic when it comes to leadership, especially after realizing how God views the process of leadership selection. As leaders, we too must learn not to be taken-in by the optics. Don't worry about public opinion. Rather, be sensitive to the Holy Spirit and learn to hear His voice when selecting leaders. Missing this key may result in the "Sauls" being chosen for leadership positions, and we will miss the "Davids."

Our Strengths Pushed To Extremes, Become Our Weaknesses

David was a man of great passion and emotion. He served the Lord with such zeal, giving it everything he had. He strove to do the right thing, which is noble. However, his emotions and passions also became his greatest liabilities. Let me explain. Recall when he and his men guarded the flocks of Nabal, while David was running from Saul. He did this without being asked. One day, when he went to Nabal seeking provisions for his men, Nabal refused. Basically, Nabal said, *"No one asked you to do this. I don't owe you anything."* David became angry. In fact, he planned to destroy Nabal and his household (See 1 Samuel 25).

Nabal's wife, Abigail, heard about it and went out to intercept David and his army. She brought provisions for them and David changed his mind. He declared to Abigail,

"Bless you for keeping me from murder and from carrying out vengeance with my own hand." (1 Samuel 25:33).

David was passionate and zealous in carrying out Saul's instructions to secure 100 foreskins of the Philistines as a dowry in order to marry his daughter. David brought back 200. When he brought the Ark of God back into Jerusalem, he led the procession with passionate zeal and dancing, worshipping the Lord with all his might. Yes, he was a man of passion. However, it was his passion that also led him to commit adultery with Bathsheba and have her husband Uriah killed.

These are just some examples to make us pause and think about the decisions we make and how we conduct ourselves as leaders. We are called to be decisive and take appropriate action when needed. However, we also need to know when not to act and wait on the Lord. We may have a passion to see some need met in ministry, but if God has not instructed us to do so, we will act in disobedience by continuing with our plans. In order to avoid making these errors, which can have serious consequences, we need to realize at least three things. Firstly, just because we *feel strongly* about something doesn't mean we should do it. Secondly, just because we *can* do something doesn't mean we should do it. If God hasn't asked us to do it, we will be acting in disobedience.

Thirdly, a leader *must be self-aware enough* to know what situations to avoid, and so prevent an emotional decision that could be ruinous. In the case of David and Bathsheba, if he went out to war that Spring, as Kings did, he wouldn't have been on his balcony to see her bathing. Had he known what things acted as "triggers" that could result in sin, he would have held himself accountable to someone who also knew what they were in order to safeguard himself.

Every leader must be careful not to allow his strengths to become his liabilities when pushed to extremes. Self-awareness will preserve a leader, and those who follow him, to a long career of victorious ministry.

Great Leaders Are Teachable

One of the traps that leaders face is to always remain teachable. This is especially true when that leader has had some years of successful accomplishments in his life. It is so easy for pride to enter the leader's heart during these times. Often, that pride will blind a leader from hearing the instructions of the Lord or the counsel of a trusted associate. Great leaders are always great students. We should never stop growing as leaders. This means we can never stop learning. We must guard against ever becoming unteachable. In the event that we do, we must be quick to repent and change direction.

I will share some examples in David's life that illustrate this quality.

When Nathan, the prophet, called David out for his sin with Bathsheba, he quickly acknowledged his sin and repented. When he numbered Israel, acting as if victory depended upon his own resources, he was rebuked by the prophet. David quickly repented and threw himself on God's mercy as He measured out discipline for him. When David brought the Ark of God back into Jerusalem, Uzzah touched it when the oxen stumbled. God struck Uzzah down dead in an instant. Even though David was angry with God when this happened, he repented. He examined the Scriptures to learn how God had instructed the Ark to be moved and followed those instructions to the letter. (See 2 Samuel 12; 1 Chronicles 21; 1 Chronicles 13.)

We never stop learning. One key in accomplishing this is to expect God to speak to you through ANYONE. When we practice this quality that the Bible calls meekness, we will go far in maintaining a steady process of growth and development as leaders.

Leaders Don't Cave-In To Pressure

In our culture, where folks measure their popularity by how many friends or likes they have on Facebook and where polls are used to skew and shape public opinion one way other another, it is often difficult to stand your ground as a leader and not be swayed by these forces.

David had an experience when running from King Saul. Saul was pursuing him, as if he were an enemy. One day, while he and his men were out fighting a battle, they returned home to discover that their families were all taken captive. Their wives and children were gone. The entire army raised their voices in painful lament, crying over this great loss. In fact, in their grief, they determined that it was all David's fault and they wanted to stone him (See 1 Samuel 30). It doesn't take much imagination to understand how these men felt or how David felt when he looked into their tear-filled eyes. The floodgates of everyone's emotions were thrown wide open, and there was no stopping it. David's family was lost as well.

The Bible tells us that, rather than cave in to the pressure of this catastrophe, David encouraged himself in the Lord. He went to Abiathar, the priest, and asked if the Lord would help him recover everything. God instructed him to go, promising that he would recover all. This is such a powerful response to the pressures facing David, and I don't want you to miss it. Here is why: in times when leaders face great pressures, emergency meetings are called and special action committees are formed. These may be necessary, but the first thing that should be done is what David did. He inquired of the Lord. He went to God first and received a word of direction for the situation. Leaders with hearts after God seek Him first, regardless of the circumstances. They know that the One who rules over all circumstances is always looking for someone through which to show Himself strong. Be that leader.

There was another event in David's life when he faced pressures at a very critical time. It was when Saul was pursuing him. Saul had gone into a cave to rest, which happened to be the very cave David was hiding in. David's advisor encouraged David to seize the moment and kill Saul. He even said that God had presented him with this opportunity, and he should take this as God's will for him. I believe that this high-pressure incident may have been just as difficult as the previous one mentioned that occurred at Ziklag. You see, it is during times in a leader's life when it is just them and God or them and a trusted friend and advisor that can be the turning point in their life. Who could have blamed David for killing Saul? Should he pass up this opportunity to avenge himself and kill his enemy? A man after God's own heart evaluates present circumstances according to a higher set of values. David refused to harm Saul because he determined that he would not touch the Lord's anointed (See 1 Samuel 24:6).

As leaders, we may never find ourselves confronted with a decision to kill our enemy or let him live. However, we may find ourselves in a place where we must choose between criticizing another leader who hurt us, treated us unfairly or even maligned us intentionally, or letting him "live." Can we bless and not curse those who may have treated us badly? Can we speak of the positive qualities of another leader who hurt us or despitefully used us? Somehow, the leader with a heart after God must find it within himself to do what David did. Though seriously flawed, leaders over us are still the Lord's anointed. Therefore, we should leave it to the Lord to deal with them.

One way that I have been helped in situations like these has been to ask myself a question, *"Will my actions be something God could bless?"* If the answer is, *"No,"* then I cannot do it. I must respond in a way so God can bless and multiply. Your decision to bless, to spare the other leader embarrassment and preserve their reputation, may mean you will stand alone. Realize, however, that you never really stand alone. If everyone is against you in your decision, God is for you. If we want to be leaders after God's own heart, we must be willing to stand alone with God rather than to stand in a crowd without Him.

We have only scratched the surface in our consideration of David's leadership qualities. Nevertheless, these few key characteristics, as we practice them, will help us advance to become leaders "after God's own heart."

Profile 7: Jesus – The Model "Un-Stuck" Leader

The Model Emotionally Healthy Leader

Key Scripture: Acts 10:38

The Apostle John wrote in his Gospel that if he wrote all the things that Jesus did, the world would not contain the books that could be written (See John 21:25). Of course, no one would dispute that. Likewise, no one book could contain all the qualities of Jesus' leadership. Therefore, I will only mention seven key qualities of Jesus' leadership that all leaders could imitate.

Before I do, I would like to make a very important observation. We must realize that Jesus did all the things He did as a result of being filled with the Spirit of God from the moment He was baptized in the Jordan by John the Baptist. In the book of Philippians, we are told that Jesus emptied and humbled Himself, taking upon himself the form of a servant. He took on our humanity. Jesus was the God/Man. However, all the demonstrations of power He performed were because of the indwelling Spirit of God. Why is this so important? Because we have the same Spirit dwelling in us. We have the mind of Christ by the Spirit. We have the ability to do the works Jesus did by the same Spirit. Christ in us is the hope of glory. In the book of Romans, Paul declares that, "If the same Spirit that raised Jesus Christ from the dead dwells in you, ... He will also enliven your mortal bodies..." (See Romans 8:11). While this may be a reference to the resurrection, I believe it also includes our mortal bodies, while ministering in His Name on earth. The bottom line is, we have the SAME Spirit dwelling in us NOW. Therefore, we have the potential to be the same kind of leader that Jesus was while on earth.

Here are several key elements practiced by the model emotionally healthy leader:

He Was A Man Of Prayer

There was no one who accomplished more in his short three and one-half years of public ministry than Jesus. He was busy. Crowds attended Him everywhere He went. In fact, there came a time in His ministry where he could no longer minister inside the city because the crowds were just too large, yet He always made time for prayer.

It is interesting that it was this element in the life of Jesus that impressed His disciples so much that they asked Him one day, *"Master, teach us to pray."* They didn't ask Him to teach them how to administrate or conduct a healing service. They didn't ask Him to teach them how to debate Pharisees and Scribes. They asked Him to teach them to pray. The fact that they asked Him this tells us that Jesus made prayer such a priority that the disciples recognized it as a defining element in His ministry. It was Jesus' prayer life that resulted in the mighty manifestations of power so evident in all Jesus did. Of course, they were correct in their assessment. Jesus prayed at night. He prayed during the day. He prayed alone. He prayed in the Synagogue and in the Temple. He prayed with His disciples. He prayed.

The emotionally healthy leader must be a person of prayer. I am not saying that he must be a person who prays. There is a difference. Prayer is something that is expected of all leaders. Leaders pray. However, when a leader is recognized as a *person of prayer*, it tells us that prayer is the defining element in the leader's life. It is not something he does: it is something he is.

Unfortunately, in trying to keep up with the hectic pace of ministry and to get things done, prayer is often sacrificed, limited or ignored completely. Many churches don't even have prayer meetings scheduled in their weekly activities. This may be evidence that prayer is not a priority in the life of the leader of that ministry. If Jesus made time for prayer, and it was what defined Him, then certainly we should do the same. Perhaps the reason why people don't come to prayer meetings anymore is because the leader has not demonstrated himself as a person of prayer. I am not trying to be critical here. I am trying to make a point. Prayer is the key to anointing and power in ministry. Prayer, in the leader and in the church, will make the ministry a *transformational* one, rather than just an *informational* one. People don't need more information; they need transformation. They don't need more religious activity; they need spiritual power.

Prayer, in the life of a leader, will accomplish great things. It will keep him intimately connected to the Father. It will produce anointing that will empower his ministry to transform lives. It will produce fruit in the ministry that will remain long after the busyness of activity and programming fades away.

He Spoke The Truth In Love

Jesus not only spoke the truth; He is the Truth. He never minced words. He never worried if He would offend His hearers. He was more concerned with not offending the Father. Whether He was speaking to publicans and sinners or to Scribes and Pharisees, Jesus spoke the truth.

Why are so many today afraid of speaking the truth? For many, truth is a relative thing. What one person believes to be true, may be very different from what another person believes. Others may not know what the truth is at all. Still others may consider selective truth as their standard. Selective truth is what people have when they accept only certain elements they consider truthful, while rejecting others. They come to the Scriptures with a set of values and pre-conceived notions. They hold the authority of these notions above the authority of the Scriptures. Rather than making their notions conform to the Scriptures, they conform the Scriptures to their notions. This practice bankrupts the Scriptures of their power. It reduces God's Word to the level of any other literary work. It denigrates the Lord, whose words they are.

Jesus spoke a certain way to publicans and sinners and another way to Scribes and Pharisees. He was gentle with sinners. Remember when the woman caught in adultery was brought to Him? He looked away from her and wrote on the ground. *"Where are your accusers?"* He asked. *"There are none,"* she said. Jesus responded, *"Neither do I accuse you. Go and sin no more."* He spoke harshly to the Scribes and Pharisees, however. He called them a brood of vipers, hypocrites and whitewashed tombs (See Matthew 23:27-28). Why? They were leaders and should have known better.

Jesus didn't edit the truth based on how His hearers would react to it. He based it on whether He was being obedient to His Father in Heaven and the written word already in the Scriptures. Furthermore, Jesus never went into an emotional tailspin when He was rejected. He also never allowed Himself to be influenced by being accepted by the people. When those in His hometown of Nazareth rejected Him, He just went on to the next towns. When the people rushed on Him to try to make Him King, he walked away. To the emotionally healthy leader, truth is not a kind of currency that is valued and devalued according to market conditions. It is something independent and absolute. Truth is a standard set by God and not the opinions of people or the winds and waves of a fickle culture. Emotionally healthy leaders speak the truth in love. Jesus loved the Father, and He loved the world. His love of the Father prevented Him from ever compromising on what truth was. His love for the people was too great for Him to alter it or water it down because they might be offended by it. May the Lord help us to do likewise.

He Maintained Healthy Boundaries

Jesus laid His life down for the world. He gave His life for His friends as a demonstration of His love for them, but *He never let anyone walk all over Him.* Jesus never committed Himself to man, because He knew what was in men's hearts. He knew people. He knows us. He knows what makes us tick. He knows what pushes our buttons. He went out of His way for people all the time. He stated, *"...no man takes my life from me. I have the power to lay it down and raise it up, for the Father gave me this authority.*" (See John 10:18). This is an important element of healthy leadership. No one should be allowed to drain you. They can come to you for help. You can make yourself available to them. You can GIVE them all of you that you chose to give. However, you must never allow them to take what you may not be giving or to do so at a rate you are not prepared or able to give. A healthy leader must learn to say, *"No."* He must also learn to say, *"That's enough."* He must learn to say; *"I'll have time for you next week in my schedule, not today."* These are personal boundaries every healthy leader must establish and maintain.

When speaking to the rich young ruler, Jesus stated the standard for following Him in answer to the man's question. *"Sell your possessions and follow me,"* Jesus said, *"Then you will have eternal life."* The man walked away, sorrowfully. Here is the boundary: **Jesus let him walk away.** You or I may have said, *"Wait, let me explain what I meant by that."* We wouldn't want him to walk away. What kind of leader lets people walk away? If we really cared, wouldn't we keep trying to explain why it is necessary to have certain boundaries and meet certain conditions? Jesus didn't do any of those things. In fact, the passage states that *"...Jesus looked at him and loved him ..."* when He gave him the answer. Love let him walk away.

He also taught that people needed to come to the Father through the door. No one can jump over the fence to come into the Kingdom. In other words, a healthy leader permits people to have access, but they must come through the door. That is, they must get to the right place, knock and wait until the door is opened. A healthy leader does not permit "gate crashing." Let me explain:

When I first started pastoring, I did a lot of counseling. My weekly schedule sometimes contained as much as thirty hours per week in counseling appointments. This was in addition to all my other responsibilities as an Associate Pastor, a husband and father. I found myself operating under the notion that if someone said they needed to see me as soon as possible, I just had to fit them into the schedule. Needless to say, this put a strain on my marriage, my family and me. One day, I called a friend who was a professional counselor to ask for an appointment. I stated it was urgent, and my wife and I needed to see him that very week. He calmly stated that he wasn't available until the following week. Despite my insistence that it was urgent, he couldn't see me. I waited and my wife and I went to see him the following week as scheduled. When we walked into his office, he asked, *"Do you realize what I did with you?"* Immediately I said, *"Yes,"* I explained, *"You made me wait for a week to see you, and I discovered that I didn't die, but survived until we could meet."* He said, *"That's what you need to do with your appointments."* Lesson learned. Healthy leaders set boundaries. They set standards and they hold those they are trying to help accountable to them.

His Identity Was Anchored In His Relationship With The Father

Jesus knew who He was. One of the most powerful characteristics for anyone to possess, especially leaders, is a secure sense of their identity. How do we define identity? We use the term often. In our present culture there are challenges and difficulties in many areas and on many levels. Opinions differ on a broad range of things we face in our culture. From religion to politics, people are being labeled by the position they maintain on an issue. We call it "identity" politics. Once we identify a person by their position, we label them by it. There is a positive and negative aspect to labeling as such. On the positive side, we can understand a person's values and mores. On the negative side, we stereotype people unfairly according to our own biases, shutting them down if we disagree with them. Doing this opens up a proverbial "can of worms" that will lead us into a destructive, downward spiral with worsening consequences.

Jesus never became mired in the polarizing forces of the culture in which He lived. People had varied opinions of Him. Some said He was a prophet: others said He was demonized. Some said He was the Messiah: others said He was a glutton and wine bibber. Talk about extremes. Yet, we always see a consistency in Jesus' message and ministry. How was He able to accomplish all He did, with all these opinions swirling around about Him? He knew who He was. This is so important for us to understand and to imitate for at least two main reasons. Firstly, because His identity was in His relationship to the Father, it was anchored in the eternal realm. It transcended the earthly realm. He never became entangled in the issues of His day or became sidetracked by what people said about Him. Because He knew who He was, He was enabled to live above all these things. As such, He was empowered to consistently speak into every situation with objective, divine wisdom and revelation. Secondly, a deep sense of security was developed within Him. He was not afraid. He was on a mission *from* His Father and *with* His Father. Therefore, He identified with the Father and partnered with Him in all He did. He was able to move toward its accomplishment steadily and in accordance with the Father's timetable.

As we mediate upon these two points, we will come to understand how powerful and important it is that we derive our identity from the Father, just as Jesus did.

In the book of Romans, the Apostle Paul uses language that identifies us with the first Adam. We are identified with his humanity and his sinful, fallen nature. Paul also uses language that identifies us with Abraham as the father of our faith. He calls us his offspring, or his descendants, and that is who we are. Just as Abraham's faith caused him to be accounted in righteous standing with God, we too are accounted the same standing by the same faith as Abraham. What about our identity in Christ, the Last Adam?

When Jesus was baptized by John in the Jordan River, something very significant happened. The heavens opened (spiritual revelation was experienced), the Spirit of God descended upon Jesus and the voice of the Father spoke, *"This is my beloved Son in whom I am well pleased."* (See Matthew 3:17). Let us unpack the significance of this event and how it applies to us.

The Apostle Paul tells us that death through sin passed upon all mankind through the first Adam. He also teaches that life passed to all who believe in and are born again through the last Adam – Jesus. In the first Adam, all die.

In the last Adam, all are made alive (See Romans 5). Likewise, in the first Adam, all of humanity is born in sin and severed from relationship to the Father. However, in Christ (the last Adam), all are made righteous and are reunited in relationship to the Father. This means that our identity is also derived from our relationship to the Father, through Jesus. Furthermore, it means that when the Father said that He was "well pleased" with Jesus, He was saying that about all the offspring of the Last Adam as well. He is well pleased with all of us *in and through* Jesus Christ, the Last Adam. This revelation will revolutionize our lives. Because our identity is in our relationship with the Father, we too can live above the opinions of others or the varied forces of our culture. We too can maintain an eternal, objective view of truth that transcends the value system of this world. We, too, can speak the truth in love to our generation with the confident assurance Jesus had when He spoke to His generation. Our leadership will not require validation from the opinions of our hearers or followers. Our validation comes from the Father as His sons and daughters. Therefore, we can lead with bold confidence, regardless of whether people agree with us and accept our message or not. We can truly be spokesmen for God, being co-laborers with Jesus for His glory.

He Was Flexible, But Uncompromising

Jesus could speak to anyone. He met with sinners and publicans, Scribes and Pharisees, men and women, adults and children. He could hold sophisticated conversations with the religious scholars of His day and speak to broken, wounded people whose lives were in shambles. Regardless of who His audience was, He never compromised. He spoke truth with the flexibility demanded by the audience and individuals He ministered to. The book of Hebrews defines Jesus as being *"... the same yesterday, today and forever..."* (See Hebrews 13:8). He was consistent. All leaders must be as well.

This quality of leadership is extremely important and has benefits to the leader and those following him. For the leader, it places him in a light that makes him dependable. People know what they are going to get when they go to this leader. For those following, they can begin to build trust because they know the leader is consistent. He is not a flip-flopper. The emotionally healthy leader doesn't shift positions depending on the winds of culture or popular opinion. He is steady, dependable, trustworthy and sound. Methodologies may need to change with the times, but values, truths and godly principles can never be compromised. We have permission to make whatever changes we need to make to lead our generation.

199

However, we are never given license to change the Biblical message or standard of truth that the Father has already established. We can and should be flexible.

We must never be compromising. Blending our values with those of this present culture serves only to weaken our message and undermine our leadership. When anything and everything can be considered true, or right, then nothing alone can be true or right. A compromised standard is no standard at all. It can shift at any moment, depending upon the prevailing winds of the day. There are many these days that believe they can lead in this way. They are mistaken. How long would you keep a watch that varied the speed of what a second was? You would discard it as undependable. Would you use a ruler that varied what a millimeter was? Of course not. We would never know what a true inch was. A ruler could be wooden, metal or a laser, but an inch is still an inch, regardless of what form is used to measure it. Let us be flexible in our leadership style and application, but also be sure to never compromise our values as leaders. As we do this, we will become trusted, blessed by the Father and followed by those He brings to us.

As mentioned above, these are just a few key elements in Jesus' leadership that we can all put into practice. As we do, we will continue to grow and develop into mature, healthy leaders. We will have a God-honoring, eternal impact on those who follow us.

Profile 8: The New You

A New Beginning And The Process Of Healing

Key Scripture: 2 Corinthians 5:17

A s you read through the profiles in this book, I am certain that there were things that you identified with. We all, at one time or another, face one or more of the challenges faced by the leaders in these profiles. As you evaluate your experience with these challenges, I want you to do so with an eye toward *degree*. You see, not all of us experience them to the same degree or at the same time. Some are experienced in combination: some independently from others. My point is that I don't want you to become alarmed simply because you identify with any of them. For example, just because you may battle insecurities as King Saul did doesn't mean that these will necessarily manifest to the same degree as it did in his life and career as a leader.

I remember taking a course in Abnormal Psychology in college. The professor issued a disclaimer in the first session. He said that every student would see something diagnosed as "abnormal" during their study that they themselves do. He warned us not to panic, but (as in these profiles) it is to the degree we experience them that will determine how much of a problem we may have to deal with, if at all. Needless to say, we all breathed a sigh of relief. Think about yourself in the same way. Evaluate the degree to which a trait you have read about applies to you, and then make any necessary adjustments.

Carefully and prayerfully evaluate if these behaviors occur only occasionally in your life or if they form a basic pattern that characterizes you. If they form a baseline, you may need to seek counsel concerning them. Even if these occur only occasionally, we must still be aware of them and make changes in the way we think, so we can eliminate them and become transformed.

Five Components To Healing and Transformation

Honesty: We must be willing to be honest and transparent. Be honest with ourself and those who are assisting us in our journey toward healing.

Truth: There is only one source of objective, eternal truth in the universe. It is found in God's word, the Bible. Everything and anything else that we have accepted as truth about ourselves must be challenged by and conform to what God says about us. This is crucial in providing us with an eternal source of truth that will lead us to total freedom.

Holy Spirit: He is the Change-Agent that will facilitate the actual transformation we are seeking. He provides the power to make the changes in our thinking and behavior in the process of healing. As we commit to do our part, we must believe that He will not fail to do His part. This process is how we will receive and maintain our transformation for the rest of our lives.

Affirming Relationship: We need to prayerfully seek out someone in our lives that we can depend on to share our journey. This person is someone who loves us unconditionally and has our best interests at heart: a person who is genuinely interested in our transformation and will walk alongside of us, through thick and thin, until we arrive at our destination. They will speak the truth to us, even if it is hard to hear, because they love us and want to see us walk in victory. You don't need many people like this in your life, but I believe that God has already provided one for each of us. Sit with that person and tell them about your struggle. Covenant with them to walk together, each being responsible for their part, until there is healing. This person could be a coach, a mentor or a close friend that won't get rattled when you tell them something about your inner struggle.

Time: This may be the most challenging component of healing. It took time to get to the place you are living in right now. It will take time to move from there to complete healing.

Make time your ally, not your enemy. Don't rush the process. Remember, the Holy Spirit will lead and guide the process with you, preparing you for each step as you move toward wholeness. Because God can *"...restore the years that the locust has eaten... "*, I believe He can also consolidate the time we will need to endure the process. The process is as important as the goal.

I encourage you to be sure to celebrate your process as you progress toward your goal of complete freedom and restoration.

Damian Smeragliuolo

The Process Of Healing

To experience the restoration and healing that God desires us to have, we must understand how the process of healing works in us. The following diagram illustrates the process:

BELIEFS >>> THOUGHTS >>> EMOTIONS >>> ACTIONS

Our beliefs give rise to the basic way we think and process information. Our basic thought life becomes the filter we use to process all we believe, resulting in our basic emotional make-up. Our basic emotional condition determines our actions. Our behavior, positive or negative, arises out of our basic emotional state.

Most counseling centers on behavior modification. In other words, when we speak with a counselor about a destructive behavior, he or she usually recommends an alternate behavior. We leave their office, determined to practice the new behavior. While that may work for a while, before long, we find ourselves repeating the former, destructive behavior again. As this cycle is repeated, we can become frustrated and give up altogether.

The reason this cycle is repeated is because we have not dealt with the root of the problem. The root exists somewhere in what we believe. The foundational beliefs we have learned through experience, what others have told us in childhood and what we have otherwise learned are formative and influence our behavior, despite our attempts to change them. Unless we deal with these beliefs, replacing them with God's truth about ourselves, we will not experience the change we desire. Will-power is just not enough to accomplish this. We must exercise an *informed will power,* equipped with new truth, that will fuel the entire process.

Renewing Our Minds

In Romans 12:2, the Apostle Paul gives us the recipe for transformation. It is the process of renewing our minds. As we renew our minds, we will come to demonstrate the good, acceptable and complete will of God in our lives.

In the process of counseling, we seek to discover patterns of behavior and the roots those patterns arose from. Often, traumatic experiences in childhood, growing up in a severely dysfunctional home and living in abusive situations over long periods of time form the basic beliefs we hold about ourselves and those around us.

I knew a woman whose mother told her constantly, *"I wish I had flushed you down the toilet when you were born.*" I met this woman when she was in her forties. This idea formed the basic opinion she held of herself. Her relationships were horrible. Why? She concluded that she was worthless and that she should expect nothing more than that. After all, she believed, *"Worthless people don't deserve to be loved."*

The process of renewing our minds requires that we identify the false belief we hold about ourselves. See what God says about us in His Word, the Bible. We must unplug the lie and plug in the truth. As we do so and mediate on the truth of what God says about us, we will be transformed. We will be empowered to live the new life that Jesus purchased for us through His cross.

If there are issues that you have identified within yourself as you read these profiles, seek the counsel of someone who can work with you in the process of renewing your mind. When you do, you will be well on your way to demonstrating the good, acceptable and complete will of God.

It is my heartfelt prayer that you will begin this new journey to a New You in faith, trusting the Lord to do His part, while never failing to do yours. Remember, the One who began a good work in you will complete it. Become the transformed leader God has called you to be and *"...go into all the world..."* to transform your community, your city, your state, your nation and the world.

CPSIA information can be obtained
at www.ICGtesting.com
Printed in the USA
FFHW011048041219
56477709-62281FF